Dead Peasants

Leif Oleson-Cormack

A Samuel French Acting Edition

SAMUELFRENCH.COM
SAMUELFRENCH-LONDON.CO.UK

Copyright © 2014 by Leif Oleson-Cormack
All Rights Reserved
Cover artwork © by Skye Oleson-Cormack

DEAD PEASANTS is fully protected under the copyright laws of the United States of America, the British Commonwealth, including Canada, and all other countries of the Copyright Union. All rights, including professional and amateur stage productions, recitation, lecturing, public reading, motion picture, radio broadcasting, television and the rights of translation into foreign languages are strictly reserved.

ISBN 978-0-573-70155-9

www.SamuelFrench.com
www.SamuelFrench-London.co.uk

For Production Enquiries

United States and Canada
Info@SamuelFrench.com
1-866-598-8449

United Kingdom and Europe
Plays@SamuelFrench-London.co.uk
020-7255-4302

Each title is subject to availability from Samuel French, depending upon country of performance. Please be aware that *DEAD PEASANTS* may not be licensed by Samuel French in your territory. Professional and amateur producers should contact the nearest Samuel French office or licensing partner to verify availability.

CAUTION: Professional and amateur producers are hereby warned that *DEAD PEASANTS* is subject to a licensing fee. Publication of this play does not imply availability for performance. Both amateurs and professionals considering a production are strongly advised to the appropriate agent before starting rehearsals, advertising, or booking a theatre. A licensing fee must be paid whether the title is presented for charity or gain and whether or not admission is charged. Professional/Stock licensing fees quoted upon application to Samuel French, Inc.

No one shall make any changes in this title for the purpose of production. No part of this book may be reproduced, stored in a retrieval system, or transmitted in any form, by any means, now known or yet to be invented, including mechanical, electronic, photocopying, recording, videotaping, or otherwise, without the prior written permission of the publisher. No one shall upload this title, or part of this title, to any social media websites.

For all enquiries regarding motion picture, television, and other media rights, please contact Samuel French.

MUSIC USE NOTE

Licensees are solely responsible for obtaining formal written permission from copyright owners to use copyrighted music in the performance of this play and are strongly cautioned to do so. If no such permission is obtained by the licensee, then the licensee must use only original music that the licensee owns and controls. Licensees are solely responsible and liable for all music clearances and shall indemnify the copyright owners of the play(s) and their licensing agent, Samuel French, against any costs, expenses, losses and liabilities arising from the use of music by licensees. Please contact the appropriate music licensing authority in your territory for the rights to any incidental music.

IMPORTANT BILLING AND CREDIT REQUIREMENTS

If you have obtained performance rights to this title, please refer to your licensing agreement for important billing and credit requirements.

DEAD PEASANTS was performed on May 26th, 2011 at the Emrys Jones Theatre in Saskatoon, Saskatchewan as part of the Saskatchewan Playwrights Centre's Spring Festival of New Plays. It was directed by Pamela Haig Bartley. The cast was as follows:

BRUCE CAFFERTY .... Tom O'Hara
MARLO CAFFERTY .... Leon Willey
GRACE ESPINOZA .... Maki Yi
DAVEY BURNETT. .... Rob van Meenen

DEAD PEASANTS is the winner of the 2012 Samuel French Canadian Playwriting Constest.

CHARACTERS

BRUCE CAFFERTY – mid-forties, male.
MARLO CAFFERTY – early-forties, male.
GRACE ESPINOZA – mid-twenties, Asian, female.
DAVEY BURNETT – twenties, male.

PLACE

A small agricultural community in Southern Alberta, Canada.

TIME

Present Day.

For Gobe

ACT I

Scene One

(Present day.)

(The breakroom of TroughKing™ Manufacturers, an animal pellet factory and mill. On the left side of the stage is a door leading to the parking lot. A framed black and white photograph of the factory's founder, William Cafferty, hangs above a bathroom door at the back of the room. A small kitchenette also lines the back wall of the room.)

(A door near the front right side of the breakroom opens onto the main floor of the factory, where a large concrete wall extends past the right side of the stage. Towards the center of this wall is a crawlspace door, which leads to an [off-stage] mixing room where large metal augers are used to churn feed. Directly above the wall is a walkway that connects to the inside of the breakroom via a ladder positioned on the stage right wall. At the center of the walkway is a control panel.)

*(**BRUCE CAFFERTY**, mid-forties, sits at a table in the center of the room, working on a book of "Stress-Free Crosswords". He wears black dress pants and a dress-shirt, loosened tie. He lights a cigarette. After a few moments, **DAVEY BURNETT**, twenties, enters. He is wearing a navy blue suit which he is just on the cusp of outgrowing.)*

BRUCE. 'Bout time.

DAVEY. Sorry. Got caught in that line and–

BRUCE. That's why I had the sense to get out of there.

DAVEY. Surprised you were able to make it up.

BRUCE. It's a pretty big deal.

DAVEY. But this is your time off, right?

BRUCE. I can take it whenever.

DAVEY. Still. Nice of you.

BRUCE. Mmm.

DAVEY. His dad was kinda hoping to meet you.

BRUCE. I bet.

DAVEY. Nah, they were alright.

BRUCE. To *you*, maybe.

(A long pause.)

DAVEY. So, uh...who'da figure Spoza'd be the kind to, uh... 'hit the slopes'?

BRUCE. What?

DAVEY. His wife. *(beat)* Chinese.

BRUCE. Oh.

DAVEY. Think he'd a mention something like that. Being married to a Chinese girl? They introduced her, I figured us for being in the wrong room.

BRUCE. I already knew.

DAVEY. That we were in the right room?

BRUCE. That she was Chinese.

DAVEY. How'd you know she was Chinese?

BRUCE. I...assumed.

DAVEY. You just go and *assume* a guy's girl is Chinese?

BRUCE. Was right, wasn't I?

DAVEY. What about that last girl I saw? What do you assume *her* for?

BRUCE. White.

DAVEY. Why not Chinese?

BRUCE. Because I've met her.

DAVEY. But otherwise you'd just assume her to be—

BRUCE. No, Just Espinoza's.

DAVEY. Just Spoza's?

BRUCE. Yes. She's the only one I'd assume to be Chinese.

DAVEY. You're a funny guy, Mr. Cafferty. *(to himself)* Assumed she's Chinese… What, you two know each other or something?

BRUCE. No.

DAVEY. Then how do you assu—

BRUCE. Just did.

(Pause.)

DAVEY. Gotta be based on something.

BRUCE. Her name. You can tell by her name.

DAVEY. Grace? That's not Chinese. There's letters.

BRUCE. It's an old name. No one normal has names like that anymore. Only old ladies and the Chinese.

DAVEY. So, what? They get over here, they gotta take the *jobs* no one wants, same with the names?

BRUCE. Something like that.

DAVEY. Funny thing to assume.

BRUCE. It's not like he's going to be married to some old lady, now, is he?

DAVEY. Not any less than a Chinese.

BRUCE. He was okay in the looks department. Guy like that doesn't have to settle for someone older.

DAVEY. Hey…

BRUCE. What?

DAVEY. Barb was older.

BRUCE. That was the last one?

DAVEY. Yeah. She was like, *three years* older.

BRUCE. How am I supposed to know that?

DAVEY. Just looking at our faces! It's *three* years.

BRUCE. Didn't pick up on that.

DAVEY. Well, now you know. *(beat)* So a guy like *me's* gotta go three years my senior—

BRUCE. No…

DAVEY. —but *Spoza*...

BRUCE. That's not what I was—With a name like 'Grace' she'd be *generations* older. Thirty years older. Forty even.

DAVEY. So?

BRUCE. So cool your jets, so. I'd assume the same for you.

DAVEY. Yeah?

BRUCE. You came in here talking about dippin' into some girl named Grace? Yes, I'd assume Chinese. More likely than some geriatric.

DAVEY. You really think I could?

BRUCE. What?

DAVEY. Land a girl like her. Grace.

BRUCE. I didn't say that.

DAVEY. You said that's what you'd assume. Me being with a girl like her. Instead of an old one.

BRUCE. All I said was it's more likely that you'd date a Chinese girl than an old woman. I didn't say anything about chances.

DAVEY. Yeah, but I already dated an old one and that's the harder one to do.

BRUCE. The less *likely* one.

DAVEY. So getting a Chinese one...if getting an old one's *harder*—

BRUCE. Not harder. Less *likely*.

DAVEY. Well, if it's less *likely*, then it's gotta be that my chances are even *better* for getting a Chinese. I already beat the odds!

BRUCE. You're an idiot.

DAVEY. I'm just saying what you said!

(**MARLO CAFFERTY**, *early-forties, enters the room. He's wearing a pair of ripped jeans and a well-worn RUSH Concert Tee.*)

MARLO. Guys...

BRUCE. Marlo. *(to* **DAVEY**) What I *said* was that I wouldn't argue with it if you told me. Expecting it to happen's a whole different story.

DAVEY. Okay. But say we found, like a...common interest or something. I talked to her a couple times when she was working at Stroudy's. She seemed, I dunno...

BRUCE. What?

DAVEY. Nice.

BRUCE. So being 'nice' is going to be your common interest?

MARLO. Who's this?

BRUCE. Espinoza's wife.

MARLO. Ah. The chink.

BRUCE. Jesus, Marlo...

DAVEY. She's *Chinese.*

MARLO. Yeah! The chink.

DAVEY. That's not right.

MARLO. *(doing the eye gesture)* "Ah so. My a-pah-row-gees".

DAVEY. Not right, man...

BRUCE. Where do you get off?

DAVEY. What?

BRUCE. You come in here cracking jokes about 'hitting the slopes' and now you're laying into him for—

MARLO. Fucker! *(smacks* **DAVEY**) You got that from me!

DAVEY. Screw you! You didn't make it up!

MARLO. Said it first, didn't I? Just the same.

DAVEY. Well, you shouldn't 'a said it. 'specially considering—

BRUCE. He *didn't* say it. *You* did.

MARLO. But *I* said it first.

DAVEY. Exactly.

MARLO. The fuck does that mean?

DAVEY. I was just repeating. I don't even know what it means.

MARLO. What, you thought it was a *compliment?*

DAVEY. No...

MARLO. Then why'd you say it, if you didn't understand?

DAVEY. Cause everyone laughed.

MARLO. So you admit it. You stole it.

DAVEY. Yeah.

MARLO. Then you're a thief.

DAVEY. Fine. But I'm no racist.

MARLO. No, you're a thief. That's way worse.

BRUCE. You're both out of line.

MARLO. Take it easy. I didn't say it 'bout her. It was a while back when we was at the 'rippers. Davey got excited about this one girl there and she was also—

BRUCE. I don't care...

MARLO. Why are we banging on about this broad, anyway?

BRUCE. Davey's got *designs*.

DAVEY. No, I don't.

MARLO. *Already*? Give it some time, man.

BRUCE. That's what he's been saying...

DAVEY. No, I didn't. It was just... It's just talk.

MARLO. After her already... Fuck that's cold. Hey! You're actually colder than *he* is right now. *(laughs)* See what I did there?

BRUCE. Clever.

DAVEY. I'm not! I was just wondering...

BRUCE. If he had a shot.

MARLO. Fucker...

DAVEY. I just wanted to know. Like, in terms of league.

MARLO. Got a better chance than Spoza. That's for sure.

BRUCE. Wait. Are you asking if you could land a girl like Grace or actually *get* Grace?

DAVEY. Doesn't matter.

MARLO. Horndog's got yellow fever!

BRUCE. Well, there's a difference. A girl like Grace is just some girl that's young and happens to be Chinese. But Grace? You two have history...

MARLO. You have *history*?

DAVEY. She served me a couple times at Stroudy's, but that's before I knew she was with Spoza.

MARLO. Were.

DAVEY. Huh?

MARLO. He's dead. You gotta say "before you knew she *were* with Spoza".

DAVEY. Were...

MARLO. With Spoza.

DAVEY. But that's all we've got in terms of history.

BRUCE. You sure about that?

DAVEY. That's as historical as we get.

MARLO. *(correcting)* 'Hysterical'.

DAVEY. That's as hysterical as we get.

BRUCE. How about the fact her husband died doing your job?

DAVEY. Oh.

MARLO. "Oh", he says.

BRUCE. That's some pretty heavy history, you ask me...

MARLO. An encyclopedia. Thirty volumes a' fuckin' Wagnalls right there.

DAVEY. I didn't have anything to do with it.

BRUCE. Who was supposed to be cleaning those augers? It was his day off.

DAVEY. I called him in to help. He was showing me.

BRUCE. And where were you?

DAVEY. I ran outta smokes. I hadda go get some.

MARLO. Press any buttons on your way out?

DAVEY. Hey. That's not cool.

BRUCE. No, what's not *cool* is that a good worker got twisted to death 'cause he had to show you how to do your fucking job.

MARLO. We lost a good worker. A *good* worker.

DAVEY. And I'm not?

MARLO. He'd a been there to stop it...

DAVEY. How do you know that?

MARLO. He don't smoke.

DAVEY. I've never cleaned the augers, how do you expect me to—

BRUCE. Super's supposed to know all the jobs. Even if he is just an assistant.

DAVEY. It was my first time! How should I a' known Marlo'd call in sick?

MARLO. Oh, so now it's *my* fault! You miserable little—

DAVEY. I'm not saying that. It's just—

MARLO. You should've known better than to promote some feedbag *fuck*...

BRUCE. I'm beginning to see that.

DAVEY. *(hurt)* I'm not a feedbager.

BRUCE. Anymore. You're not a feedbager *anymore*. And we'll see about that.

MARLO. Yeah.

(Pause. **DAVEY** *starts to fight back tears. He gets up and turns away from the guys.)*

MARLO. *(to* **BRUCE***)* When'd you guys get back?

BRUCE. Just now. Went on forever.

MARLO. Sorry you had to go it alone. But I knocked off around four, so there's no way I'd be getting up that early for free.

BRUCE. I didn't expect you to—

*(***DAVEY** *begins to snivel loudly)*

What is that? Is he—

MARLO. Oh boy.

BRUCE. Christ, Davey...

MARLO. Fuckin' kids. *(hands him a paper towel)* Here, hide your face in that.

BRUCE. Guy's got a hard-on the entire funeral, but call him a feedbager *once* and he starts—

DAVEY. Shut up.

(Beat.)

BRUCE. What did you say? *(to* **MARLO***)* You believe this? *Feedbag* just told me to shut up.

MARLO. Feedbag's too good for him. I think *Pallet Boy's* a better fit.

DAVEY. *(whining)* No...

MARLO. Then watch yourself.

DAVEY. All I'm saying is I'm not the only one with history. We all got it.

MARLO. I wasn't even there!

BRUCE. That's his point.

MARLO. Yeah? Well, neither were you.

BRUCE. It's my week off. I'm not supposed to.

MARLO. You're the one who promoted Davey. None of this woulda happened if—

BRUCE. So it's *my* fault?

MARLO. *I'm* not the one that killed him.

BRUCE. So me? Is that what you're saying?

MARLO. *He's* the one saying it.

DAVEY. I didn't—no. The place did. The augers or whatever.

MARLO. And me and Bruce own the place, so—

DAVEY. I'm just saying there's history. Just as much as there is with me. *(beat)* Maybe more.

BRUCE. You don't know what you're talking about.

MARLO. Really starting to think it was him that pressed that button...

DAVEY. Fuck you. If it starts anywhere, it's with your hung-over ass.

MARLO. Are you *serious?*

BRUCE. Alright...

MARLO. Keep crying, ya' little shit.

DAVEY. We had to go in there 'cause *you* called in sick.

MARLO. *(moving towards him)* Get up. Get the fuck up!

BRUCE. *(loudly)* I *said* alright! *(pause)* No one's to blame, okay? *(beat) Okay?*

(The sound of a work buzzer.)

MARLO. Fine. Whatever.

DAVEY. I'm sorry. But you're the ones pointed fingers.

BRUCE. Get out.

DAVEY. Me?

BRUCE. You heard the bell. It's your shift.

DAVEY. I thought we were just having a meeting tonight. On account of the funeral an' all. I still needta walk Baby.

BRUCE. Someone has to scrub that floor.

DAVEY. I'm all dressed up.

BRUCE. So change. You want to be anything more than a *feedbager...*

DAVEY. This is all I got.

BRUCE. Then wear it over. *(clapping his hands)* Hurry up! You're on the clock.

DAVEY. I'll just... Okay.

*(**DAVEY** grabs an oversized blue coverall from the wall and wears it over his suit. His tie dangles outside of it.)*

DAVEY. Well, uh, let me know what you guys think about the schedule. I could take some extra shifts if—

BRUCE. Go.

DAVEY. Okay. *(to **MARLO**)* Sorry.

*(**DAVEY** grabs a stereo lying on the kitchenette and begins to leave.)*

BRUCE. What's this?

DAVEY. I figured since you guys never use it...

BRUCE. We're paying you to *work*.

MARLO. Ah, let 'im have it. *(beat)* Go ahead, kid.

DAVEY. Thanks.

> *(***DAVEY** *exits the breakroom, heading towards the crawlspace. He sets down his cassette player next to it and exits stage right.)*

MARLO. You think one of us should go down there? Make sure everything's okay 'til we hear back from Eddle?

BRUCE. Nah. Let's play a bit. Grab the chips. *(grabs a deck of cards and begins to shuffle)* Twenty dollar pot. You deal.

MARLO. Sure you wanna do that? Could just play for fun.

BRUCE. After this week?

MARLO. Fine by me.

> *(***MARLO** *pulls a flask from his pocket and pours it into his coffee cup.* **BRUCE** *deals.)*

MARLO. You sure we got nothing on Spoza?

BRUCE. No. Just him.

MARLO. So...?

BRUCE. Nothing.

MARLO. Fuck *me*.

> *(***DAVEY** *returns from stage right. He is carrying a backpack and bucket. He opens the crawlspace door, squeezes inside, and pulls the bucket in after him.)*

MARLO. Alright, gimme another. *(***BRUCE** *gives him a card.)* Again. *(***BRUCE** *gives him another,* **MARLO** *smiles triumphantly)* Ah?

BRUCE. All yours.

> *(Pause.)*

MARLO. Shoulda been him...

BRUCE. Think I don't know that?

MARLO. And now, with him going on about Grace?

BRUCE. I know...

MARLO. God*damn*, it shoulda been him.

(Lights fade.)

Scene Two

(TITLE: TWO YEARS EARLIER.)

(**MARLO***'s apartment. Burce is lying on a couch/futon.* **MARLO** *comes in, holding two glasses of scotch-whiskey. He hands one to Bruce.*)

MARLO. There ya go. Hey: Happy *Ballentine's* day.

BRUCE. What?

MARLO. Joke. Name of the–fuck it. *(beat)* How long you been up now?

BRUCE. Since I started? Ten days.

MARLO. I mean sleep. You look like shit.

BRUCE. It was a...long night.

MARLO. That's why we put that couch in the breakroom, y'know.

BRUCE. I can't have the workers see me sleep.

MARLO. I'm not sayin' take your pants off. Just a nap.

BRUCE. It doesn't look good.

MARLO. Dad did that all the time. Who d'ya have working today?

BRUCE. I don't know their names yet. The Hispanic one. Gary, uh...

MARLO. Spoza? What're you trying to impress him for?

BRUCE. It's not about—It's about setting an example. If they see us sleeping—

MARLO. What *we* do ain't a part of it. You need to start learning what it means to be a boss.

BRUCE. I've *been* a boss.

MARLO. Renting cars at the airport? That's no boss.

BRUCE. I hired and fired.

MARLO. Then someone fired you, right?

BRUCE. Downsized.

MARLO. Well, the guy who did that? That's a boss. An' probably not even him. Those places are so messed you don't know who the fuck's in charge. That's why what we got here's a thing of beauty. All of it ends with us. *(beat)* Hey: *(raises glass)* To Dad.

BRUCE. I need your help.

MARLO. Clink and we'll talk. *(they clink glasses)* Don't count 'less you drink it. *(*BRUCE *drinks)* They ever let you sleep at that car place?

BRUCE. I wouldn't if they let me. It's not professional.

MARLO. 'Professional'? *(chuckles)* Professional's just people tryin' to hide how much they suck. You put me in an office like I am right now, *everyone's* gonna know I'm the king. You know why?

BRUCE. Why?

MARLO. 'Cause of my clothes. I got a style.

BRUCE. Okay...

MARLO. But 'cause those pussies don't wanna deal with one guy bein' better than the rest, they go an' make *everyone* dress the same. Playing penguins. And then– *then* they try 'an change the way you think! You got anything interesting to say, those fuckers go 'an call it 'inappropriate'. Pretty soon everyone's the same kind of shitty. Professional? *(snorts)* Fucking *communism* is what *that* is.

BRUCE. Communism...

MARLO. And if *that*'s what you're thinking of bringin' in here, you might as well head back to the city.

BRUCE. That's what I want to talk to you about.

MARLO. What?

BRUCE. Going back to the city.

MARLO. You're off in four days.

BRUCE. Yes, but... I need to go now. Like, *right* now.

MARLO. Well, hey, I'd like to help, but I'm moving into the new pad tomorrow and—

BRUCE. I'm serious. I *need* to leave.

MARLO. It's four days, Bruce. Then you got two whole weeks back home.

BRUCE. Two weeks isn't enough. I... I can't take being on my own like this.

MARLO. If you're not gonna move up here, that's the only way it's gonna work.

BRUCE. I've started again.

MARLO. Started?

BRUCE. Yeah.

(Pause.)

MARLO. How much we talking?

BRUCE. Eight thousand.

MARLO. You need to stay away from those places.

BRUCE. What I need is to be with my family. That's what kept me off it so long. Every time I'd come home, I'd see the kids and see what I had to lose. Up here it's like they don't even exist.

MARLO. If you're gonna go on about selling you can forget it. Half of this is mine.

BRUCE. Then buy me out.

MARLO. Wish I could.

BRUCE. You *just* bought a house.

MARLO. Yeah, I *just* bought a house. How much do you think that costs?

BRUCE. You could sell it.

MARLO. You think I'm gonna sell my place just 'cause you like to play cards? You want your family so bad, bring 'em up.

BRUCE. Carol has a job. A *real* job.

MARLO. Get her to quit. You're the one supposed to be making money.

BRUCE. We want the kids to have opportunities.

MARLO. We got plenty of those here. Heck, when they get a little older, we could give 'em a job at the factory.

BRUCE. That's not an opportunity.

MARLO. It's good work! *(beat)* What? *(pause)* Alright, how 'bout this? We pull a guy off the floor—Yeah... We take a guy who's been around a while—Spoza, maybe—and get 'im to run things instead of you. You pay him outta your end and just take whatever's on top. That way you can go back to the city, get another job...

BRUCE. There aren't any other jobs. And we *need* that money.

MARLO. Well, fuck! I don't know... Just tell her you're gonna lose more here than you are there.

BRUCE. If she found out I started again, that'd be it for us. Over.

MARLO. She wouldn't drop you over that.

BRUCE. She would. No. She has made that *very* clear.

MARLO. Fucking told you that bitch was a bitch...

BRUCE. Hey!

MARLO. My wrong?

BRUCE. She has this idea that if I came up and ran things a while, we might turn the place around. That way, we could pay her parents back and put all that behind us. You should see the looks they give me. The way they ask me how I'm '*doing*'? And I *know* her mother's still saying things to her. No, if Carol found out about this—

MARLO. Okay. Look, I just sold Dad's truck for six grand. If you need money that bad...maybe...*maybe* I could lend you five.

BRUCE. I lost eight.

MARLO. Tell her you paid the motel in advance. Say they gave you a discount or something.

BRUCE. Then how do I pay for the motel?

MARLO. You think you're gonna stay in a *motel* when you're off owing me five grand? Nah-uh. You're living here.

BRUCE. Great...

MARLO. What? You think you deserve better? No rent and I'll be gone tomorrow. You can even keep the futon.

BRUCE. No, you're right. That's actually very generous.

MARLO. But if I *do* that, I don't want you going out tryin' to win it back.

BRUCE. I'll go to a meeting tomorrow. Soon as I get off.

MARLO. Okay. That's uh, good. The first step is, uh, yeah... going to one of those or something. Think of it this way: If I can beat the booze, you can beat this.

BRUCE. You're not sober.

MARLO. Was for two years.

BRUCE. When?

MARLO. Ninety...six? Yeah. Ninety-six to ninety-eight. Not a single fucking drop.

BRUCE. How'd you manage that?

MARLO. Found something better to do. Started seeing this girl. Clara. Fucking amazing.

BRUCE. Yeah?

MARLO. I don't like to use the word 'love', but there were times she had me feeling like a total fag. All mushy and shit... You believe that? Me! *(beat) Shit...*

BRUCE. I wish I could've seen that.

MARLO. Better times...

BRUCE. What happened between you two?

MARLO. Killed herself. Drugs.

BRUCE. Oh. I'm sorry. Did she—

MARLO. Don't really want to talk about it. *(pause)* The point is, once you get something to keep yourself busy you'll be fine.

BRUCE. Right.

MARLO. You should check out the gun range. Great way to blow off steam.

BRUCE. I'm not really a 'gun guy'.

MARLO. Nah, you're probably looking for something a bit more 'city mouse'. There's this German broad 'bout a block down? Teaches *yoga* in her basement. Maybe that's more your style.

BRUCE. Go fuck yourself.

MARLO. *(laughs)* There he is! Hey: how about another?

BRUCE. Bring the bottle.

MARLO. Now that's what I like to hear!

(Lights fade.)

Scene Three

(Present Day.)

(The factory floor. **DAVEY** *elbows his way out of the crawlspace. He grabs his backpack sitting next to the crawlspace and pulls out a sheet of paper. He looks towards the breakroom area, then pulls a cassette from his pocket. He places it in the stereo and hits the record button.)*

DAVEY. Okay, Hi. This is Dave, Davey Burnett. I'm, the, uh, assistant supervisor here at TroughKing Manufacturers. I've been here about two years and up til' now everything's been pretty good. But that's not—What I want to do is clear things up about what happened the other day. I mean, I know I sort of fucked everything up when I—I'm sorry, I hope that's not... Yeah. Better not.

*(***DAVEY*** rewinds the tape a quick second, takes a moment to think and resumes recording.)*

Yes. Okay. You might've noticed there was a break in the tape there, but I want to make clear that it was not because I said anything confessional. All I did was swear a little and I'm sorry. Even though you didn't hear it. I know for a fact you guys don't like it when people swear 'cause my buddy Marlo got pulled over for speeding this one time and he swore at the guy and even though he wasn't drinking at all, you guys went and gave him a DUI. *(beat)* Now, I'm pretty sure you wouldn't add fake charges to something real important like this, but I don't want to take any chances and piss you guys off. I mean, I really don't want this to go up to murder instead of manslaughter just 'cause I swore and you didn't even hear it. That's not what I—Shit. *(beat)* I just want to say that that right there was also not a confession, because I know at this point I'm only a suspect and I'd like to stay that way and not be a murderer or, uh, slaughterer in your heads. Because that's all I am. A suspect. Not a murderer. Or slaughterer. I just want to say some extra stuff I didn't have the chance to say this morning because of feelings and all that.

(**DAVEY** *takes a deep breath and pulls out a piece of paper from his jacket pocket. He reads from it, occasionally digressing off-page.*)

Hello. *(beat)* Now, I agree that it's true that you gotta lotta evidence since I was the only other guy 'round at the time and it was my fingerprint that was last on the button, so I totally get why you'd think that it was me—were me— 'specially since I started to lose it when you guys asked me those last couple questions. But I thought it over and I just want to say that yes, you do have a good case and you're right, if I did confess—which I'm not doing— everything would go a lot faster and people would probably be less mad at me, but I didn't do it and I'm not a liar. *(off page)* No, Constable Jameson, I am not a liar even though you seem to think so and called me as such yesterday. I am a truther and that is all. Okay. *(on page)* And that's why I'm sending you this tape so you can add it to the end of the last one to make sure the record goes straight. I do not have anything to say about the button since I did press it, but that was before Spoza even got here 'cause he said it's a good way to get the gunk off before cleaning. So the only thing I can say about that is maybe someone else did it after me and didn't use their hands or wore gloves like they sometimes do in the movies. And I know that is not what you want to hear since that probably means a lot more work for you, but I will even talk to one of those machines you have—if I need to—because that is how strongly I feel about this. Also, I do not know if gloves leave prints, but maybe this is something you could look into? Thanks.

(**DAVEY** *pulls out another page.*)

I would now like to speak directly to Constable Jameson, so please call her into the room if she is not already there. I will wait. *(a very long pause)* Hello Constable Jameson. This is Davey Burnett, assistant supervisor at TroughKing™ Manufacturers and suspect. *(deeper voice)* Hello. *(beat)* When we were talking this morning you said you couldn't figure out why I'd do it and you're right to think that, because there is no reason. Cause I didn't. I liked Mr. Spoza more than anything, even though he didn't talk to me for almost a month after I got promoted to supervisor, but I understood that and respected his silence since he's been here two years more than me an' probably deserved it a lot better. *(off page)* And I'm not just saying that 'cause he's dead! The whole thing came out of nowhere and if anyone got it, it shoulda been him. See? That's how much I don't hate him, the fact that I'm saying that. Now, I probably shoulda told him that at the time and everything woulda been okay—I mean, not him dying, since I had nothing to do with that—he'd still be dead—but he wouldn't have hated me as much and I probably wouldn't be a suspect like I am now...But yeah. Things sorta got ahead of me and there was nothing I could do about it. Like this promotion. What happened was, Mr. Cafferty came in one day and says he wants to make me assistant super, which is big news since up 'til now that's never been a thing. So he goes and makes this big thing of it and even brings in this insurance guy to check my heart and everything. And everyone wants to know why they're checking me and only me, and Bruce says that it's so the company can make a bit of money in case anything happens to me. And then Spoza's like, "What, I'm not worth anything?" And Mr. Cafferty says no, which is kind of shitty for me since Spoza's already pissed and that just makes it worse. So then the insurance guy goes an' makes this big speech about how I'm so high up in the company that I'm just as important as the augers or the mill and if they lost any of us, the place would be in big trouble which is why they need to be covered in case any of us break down. Then Spoza cracks this joke about how I'm probably worth the least since the mill and the augers have bigger brains. Which is also not true, since I'm worth more than both of them. Like together. And they don't have brains, so that shows how much he knows. But yeah. Everyone laughed at Spoza's joke and I started to cry a little and then everyone laughed at that, so that's when I gave up on trying to make him feel better. I mean, it was a mean thing for him to say. There was also this one time, back when I first started working here, that he came up and punched me in the back of the head for no reason. Wouldn't even say why! So I didn't feel like it was my job to try an' cheer him up. But I just want to say that even though I called him a bad word... *(whispering)* the 'A' one *(normal)* that is not a reason for me to kill him. Because I didn't. I mean, what? I'm just going to kill him over some joke? Or a punch? No. (beat) What I'm saying is...uh... *(looks through the pages again, finds his place and begins reading)* Yes. Mr. Spoza had much more reason to kill me than I had to kill him. But he didn't and that is too bad, because now I am a suspect and he is dead when it should be the other way around. (pause) I think I should also say that since Spoza didn't kill me and had a reason to, it'd be even less likely that I woulda killed him since I have no reason and that pretty much wrecks your case. So, there: I have no reason to do it and you will never find one, which would mean I would have to be a *(focusing intensely on the page)* so-ci-o-path if I did, and you already know that this is not the case since sociopaths don't cry when they are being asked questions by the police and are never careful to watch their language like I have been so far. *(beat)* So, I am sorry that I did not work out for you as a suspect, but that is sometimes how things turn out. I would just like to add that I really respect what you all do and I'm thinking of giving it a shot myself one day if you'll let me. Thank you very much and I wish you all the beast—*(correcting)* best. This is Davey Burnett. *(pause)* Goodbye.

*(***DAVEY*** ejects the tape and places it in his backpack. Lights fade.)*

Scene Four

(TITLE: TWO YEARS EARLIER.)

(Night. A parking lot. **GRACE ESPINOZA**, *an Asian woman in her twenties, stands next to a garbage can holding a styrofoam cup. She pulls out a cigarette and draws a light from a book of matches. In the process, she accidentally lights the entire book ablaze.)*

GRACE. Shit.

(She quickly draws a puff and drops the fire in a garbage can. It continues to burn.)

GRACE. Fuck...

*(**GRACE** dumps her coffee into the garbage. **BRUCE** enters through the door, also carrying a cup of coffee.)*

BRUCE. Are you, uh, 'protesting' something?

GRACE. What?

BRUCE. It's a joke. You're throwing out good coffee.

GRACE. It's not good.

BRUCE. Oh. *(takes a sip)* Hey, you're right. *(beat)* I just meant like those tea party guys. Back in the day they would—

GRACE. That was tea. I threw out coffee.

(Pause.)

BRUCE. Do you, uh, happen to have a light?

GRACE. Last one.

BRUCE. Oh.

GRACE. We could butt fuck.

BRUCE. Oh. I, uh...

GRACE. You light yours off my butt. *(beat)* The tip of my cigarette?

BRUCE. Oh, right! *(searches his pockets)* I think I'm all out. Do you have any extra...

(GRACE sighs. She reaches into her pockets and grabs her pack. As she does this, a pain hits her and she grabs her stomach, letting out a slight groan.)

BRUCE. You alright?

GRACE. Just heartburn.

BRUCE. Oh.

(She pulls out a cigarette and holds the tip of it against the lit end of her smoke.)

GRACE. Go ahead. Breathe in.

*(**BRUCE** grabs the smoke and slowly inhales. He chokes, coughing in her face.)*

GRACE. Jesus!

BRUCE. Sorry. It's been a while since I... Sorry.

(He goes in for another breath, still holding the cigarette to hers. She pulls away.)

GRACE. I think you're lit.

BRUCE. Oh. Thanks.

*(A long pause. **GRACE** watches as **BRUCE** continues to struggle with the smoke.)*

GRACE. Okay, what is this? You're no smoker.

BRUCE. I am. *(waves cigarette, stifles a cough)* See?

GRACE. You might be smok-*ing* but you're not a smok-*er*.

BRUCE. I'm trying to start.

GRACE. You're *trying* to start?

BRUCE. Yeah. Everyone I know seems to do it, so I just figured...

GRACE. You're going to start smoking as a goof?

BRUCE. Why'd you start?

GRACE. I don't know. It looked cool.

BRUCE. Oh. So it 'looked cool'?

GRACE. Okay...

BRUCE. So, *basically*–   **GRACE.** I get it.

BRUCE. A goof.

GRACE. Fine. We're both goofs.

BRUCE. I'm Bruce.

GRACE. Grace.

BRUCE. Nice to meet you.

GRACE. *(re: cigarette)* They're good if you want to get away from people and not look sad. That's the real reason I started.

BRUCE. 'Cause you're sad?

GRACE. 'Cause I *looked* sad. In high school.

BRUCE. Everyone looks sad in high school.

GRACE. Everyone *is* sad in high school. That's when you're supposed to pick it up, not...*(gestures towards him) this.*

BRUCE. I'm a late bloomer.

GRACE. My boyfriend was a drummer in this band and I had to go to, like, every one of their shows. Anyways, I hated being around them 'cause they would always call me, like, "Yoko" and shit. Not because I was a Yoko, they were just like, "hey we're in a band and she's Asian, so…"

BRUCE. Right.

GRACE. And none of my friends would go with me because they kind of sucked and probably *should* have broken up—I tried telling him—and I'd spent most of my time outside. But, if you don't smoke you just look like you're waiting for a ride from your parents so...yeah.

BRUCE. I guess you were one of the 'cool' kids, then.

GRACE. Hardly.

BRUCE. Dating a guy in a band sounds pretty cool.

GRACE. *(snorts)* Not if he treats you the same as his drums.

BRUCE. Priorities out of whack, huh?

GRACE. That's not what I said. *(beat)* What do you *do* to a drum?

BRUCE. I don't know...you hit it with those...uh, the sticks.

GRACE. Take out the sticks and you've got it.

(Pause.)

BRUCE. He *hit* you?

GRACE. *(nonchalanty)* Rimshot.

BRUCE. Oh my god, that's just—

GRACE. Let's not go and make a big thing of it.

BRUCE. Well it *is* a big thing. A really big thing. Anyone who would—

GRACE. Honestly, the music was a lot more painful.

BRUCE. So is that why you're here? Because he, uh...hit you?

GRACE. *(laughs)* Why would I go to Addicts Anonymous for that?

BRUCE. I don't know. It's not something you want in your life.

GRACE. Yeah, but it's not a—What would my addiction be? Fists?

BRUCE. I dunno.

GRACE. No one's addicted to fists. Except maybe that Charlotte slut. *(they both laugh)* It's true! You know she's only here to meet people, right?

BRUCE. She seemed pretty sincere to me.

GRACE. She wouldn't tell people she was a sex addict if she was. She'd just make something up about drugs and talk around it.

BRUCE. I don't see how—

GRACE. You got this room fulla desperate guys trying to drop shit and there she is, talking about how *badly* she needs to get laid. How she "aches" for it. Who's *not* gonna try and give that a shot? It'd be like if they made you do yours in a room fulla bookies. Look around when she talks about her next slip. There's always one guy who looks a little more uncomfortable than he should be.

BRUCE. I'll keep an eye out for that.

GRACE. You should. Best part of the show.

BRUCE. So what do you do, exactly?

GRACE. *(sharply)* I *have* a boyfriend.

BRUCE. Oh. Did you go to school for that, or–

GRACE. I'm just letting you know before you say something.

BRUCE. I'm not trying to— I have a wife.

GRACE. Well, we're married too. So...yeah. *(beat)* I'm a waitress.

BRUCE. What kinda job is he?

GRACE. He's taking correspondence classes for law, but right now he makes animal pellets at some shithole outside of town.

BRUCE. TroughKing?

GRACE. You know it?

BRUCE. I own it. Well, half. My brother and I...

GRACE. I didn't mean to call it a—

BRUCE. I know what it is. Which one is he?

GRACE. Gary Espinoza.

BRUCE. Oh, right. No, I should've guessed.

GRACE. Why should you have *guessed*?

BRUCE. Just because...I don't know.

GRACE. What? 'Cause we're both ethnic?

BRUCE. No. *(pause)* Well, maybe, but—

GRACE. You think that's how it works? We just saw each other on the street one day and figured 'Hey, we're both *not*–white. Let's breed.'

BRUCE. I'm sorry. I didn't mean to be...

GRACE. It's not even like we're the same race!

BRUCE. I'm an idiot, okay? Please forgive me. *(**GRACE** chuckles)* What?

GRACE. Your city stripes are really showing. You all bullshit the same way. Act more polite than you mean.

BRUCE. I *was* raised here.

GRACE. Sure don't act like it.

BRUCE. Thank you.

GRACE. So you're one of *those*. Why'd you come back if you're so good?

BRUCE. My dad left us the factory when he died.

GRACE. And you had nothing *better* going on in the Great Big City, so...

BRUCE. Pretty much.

GRACE. Does that mean you're the Trough King?

BRUCE. That was my dad. My brother and I are just, uh... trough princes.

GRACE. Well if he's dead, someone's gotta take the throne.

BRUCE. Marlo can have it.

GRACE. Wow...giving up on the Trough Kingdom... How will the common folk take to this?

BRUCE. Fine. It's me, then. *I'm* the Trough King. *(loudly)* I, Bruce Cafferty, am the King of *all* Troughs!

GRACE. Yes! Own it!

BRUCE. *(even louder)* The ruler of *all* that is trough!

GRACE. Okay, take it easy...

BRUCE. *(shouting)* A commoner has no right to speak that way to a king!

(They both laugh.)

BRUCE. So why are you here?

GRACE. Huh?

BRUCE. Your addiction. You never talk inside. And it's pretty obvious you're not here for the coffee...

GRACE. Guess.

BRUCE. Nah-uh. No way I'm getting into that.

GRACE. C'mon. It'll be fun. No one else knows. Not even Doggins. Just don't call me Yoko.

BRUCE. Okay...uh...alcohol?

GRACE. No way I'm giving that up.

BRUCE. Smoking?

GRACE. Ditto.

BRUCE. I don't know. Heroin.

GRACE. Whoa! Jumping into the big time!

BRUCE. There's no way I can win with this, can I?

GRACE. It's not a drug.

BRUCE. Well, 'Everything can be a drug if you let it run your life.'

GRACE. You know what I mean.

BRUCE. Gambling?

GRACE. Nope.

BRUCE. Eating disorder?

GRACE. No, but thank you. Unless you meant the other kind.

BRUCE. There's no way I could think that.

(Pause.)

GRACE. Guess again.

BRUCE. That pretty much does it.

GRACE. There's no other addictions you could *possibly* think of?

BRUCE. The, uh, the Charlotte thing?

GRACE. Not exactly, but...yeah. Sort of.

BRUCE. That's nothing to be ashamed of. Probably the best one to have, really! Long as you're safe...

GRACE. I shouldn't have said anything.

BRUCE. I didn't mean to sound—

GRACE. I'm just trying to figure things out, okay? I don't have many people to talk to and with Gary working 12 hour days and his classes... I've never cheated. It's just...you know...*tempting*.

BRUCE. I know what you mean. I have to come up here every two weeks to run the place and when I'm back home I'm fine, but here? It's like I'm not even me anymore.

GRACE. Or you're *too* you.

BRUCE. Yeah...

(Pause.)

GRACE. We should probably head back.

BRUCE. Hey... .what if we went out for some *real* coffee? The good kind.

GRACE. Oh, uh...

BRUCE. Just friends, of course. I think maybe if we both had someone to talk to... I mean, you don't talk in there, so...

GRACE. Gary's picking me up at nine.

BRUCE. I'll have you back at quarter to.

(Pause.)

GRACE. Half past?

BRUCE. I'll drive.

(They walk away together. Lights out.)

Scene Five

(Present day.)

*(The breakroom. **MARLO** and **BRUCE** are finishing a game of poker. In front of **MARLO** is a large stack of chips, while **BRUCE** only has a few.)*

BRUCE. All in.

MARLO. Call. *(beat)* Got here pretty quick, didn't we?

BRUCE. Just go.

*(**MARLO** grabs a few chips and slides them forward.)*

BRUCE. Two pair.

MARLO. Straight.

*(**BRUCE** sighs.)*

Shoulda paced yourself...

BRUCE. Okay, I don't need tips from a—

MARLO. What? A *winner*?

BRUCE. Just...*Don't*.

*(**BRUCE** exits to the bathroom, closing the door behind him. A slight pause followed by the sounds of smashing.)*

MARLO. Jesus Chri—

(The phone rings.)

Hey! Keep it down.

*(**MARLO** walks over and answers the phone.)*

MARLO. TroughKings. *(pause, more crashing)* Actually, he's kinda busy right now. But we were wondering when we're gonna be seeing something out of this Spoza deal. *(pause)* No, I get that, but the thing was—the thing *was* we wanted *everyone* covered. Not just the kid. *(pause)* I don't care *what* he told you, that's what we *wanted*. *(pause)* Well, you go tell them that and—Hey. HEY! Customer's always right, ain't he? Customer's *always* right. What are they gonna say to that? *(long pause)* Oh. *(beat)* Well how 'bout some of that worker's comp shit? I heard when stuff like this happens they sometimes give out—*(pause)* Well, you *make* sure. *(pause)* Yeah, Grace. What about her? *(long pause)* Bullshit. How much does she want? *(pause)* Un-be-fucking-lievable. *(long pause)* Yeah, I'll tell him. And, uh, keep us posted on all the...yeah.

(**MARLO** *hangs up the phone.*)

That ungrateful little—

(The sound of more crashing.)

Hey!

(**MARLO** *walks over and kicks the bathroom door.* **BRUCE** *shrieks. Lights out.*)

Scene Six

(TITLE: ONE YEAR EARLIER)

(MARLO's apartment. Center stage is a futon. There is a dresser on stage right. GRACE and BRUCE are in bed together.)

BRUCE. *(as if saying 'I love you')* You make me feel like a faggot.

GRACE. What?

BRUCE. You heard me. You make me feel like a faggot.

GRACE. What? Like I make you want to fuck guys?

BRUCE. No. Not like in some gay way. I just mean the feelings you give me. It makes me want to be able to write you poetry and stuff. 'Your boobs are like the moon...' Something like that. You know...pretty.

GRACE. That is the ugliest thing anyone's ever said to me.

BRUCE. Well that's 'cause I'm not a fag. But that's what I'm saying. You make me wish I were one, so I could do something that actually *is* pretty to make you get what's going on in here. But only for a minute or two, so I could go back to, well...this.

GRACE. Most people just say 'I love you'.

BRUCE. That's not what this is about.

GRACE. Oh.

BRUCE. Not like—I just don't think a word like that does it justice. I mean, I use it all the time at home with Carol and the kids, but this—

GRACE. Do you bring me up with them?

BRUCE. No...

GRACE. Then pay me the same respect. You don't hear me talking about Gary.

BRUCE. Jesus! I'm trying to pay you a compliment, if you'd listen. I'm saying I don't get any of this at home. Not from Carol. Not even the kids.

GRACE. I fucking hope not.

BRUCE. Not *that*. Just what it's like when we're together. Not even in a sex way. It's...it's better than love. It's just this feeling of... I don't even know what it is.

GRACE. Now that...*(kisses him)* Might be one of the nicest things, anyone's ever said to me. You *faggot*.

BRUCE. Alright...

GRACE. This is what it should be like all of the time.

BRUCE. Yeah.

GRACE. Just think: once you sell that dump we'll be able to do whatever we want.

BRUCE. Well, that's *if* we can sell it. Marlo isn't exactly on board.

GRACE. Then just sell your half.

BRUCE. I'm trying to, but every time I bring someone in he spends the whole time pointing out all the problems the place has. How the machines are old, things not being up to code... It's like he *wants* me to stay. I think he knows that if it were anyone else, he might have to put in some actual effort. "And we can't have that..."

GRACE. What will we do if you can't sell?

BRUCE. I guess we'll just have to keep things the way they are.

GRACE. I don't want to keep things the way they are.

BRUCE. Do you really think you could leave Gary?

GRACE. It's not like the six hours he spends sleeping next to me count for much. And now he's saying he doesn't *know* if he wants to be a lawyer any more. What, like you *know* you want to make animal pellets your whole life? *(beat)* Oh, and get this: he wants to get *"the band"* back together.

BRUCE. Spoza plays an instrument?

GRACE. Drums. Remember? That's how I started smoking. They called me Yoko?

BRUCE. Oh.

GRACE. What?

BRUCE. I just–I didn't realize that was him.

GRACE. Of course it was. He's the only guy I've ever been with besides you.

BRUCE. Right.

(Pause.)

GRACE. Have you ever thought about burning it down?

BRUCE. What?

GRACE. The factory.

BRUCE. Every time I show up.

GRACE. I mean for the insurance. That way you wouldn't have to sell it.

BRUCE. They have ways of knowing.

GRACE. You've looked into it?

BRUCE. I want outta here just as much as you. Look, I'll figure something out.

GRACE. Good. 'Cause I'd run off with you in a second. Even if you *are* a fag.

BRUCE. You're not going to let that one go, are you?

GRACE. Nope. *(she kisses him)* I love you.

BRUCE. I think we've already established that 'I love you' is sort of a weak—

GRACE. Fine... "Your balls are like the moon."

BRUCE. Okay... But, I mean... I *did* say I was a—

GRACE. So, what? You want me to say I'm a lesbian?

(BRUCE laughs)

Oh... I get it. This whole thing was just some trick to get me to say that. A bitta jerk off fantasy for when you're back home?

BRUCE. *(playfully)* I have *no idea* what you're talking about.

GRACE. Fine, Mr. Cafferty. You got me. You've turned me into a lezzer. I've become a big fat fucking bulldyke with an unquenchable thirst for pussy!

(MARLO enters from the front door.)

MARLO. Looks like you're in the wrong bed, then.

(**GRACE** *screams.*)

BRUCE. What the hell, Marlo?

MARLO. *(to* **GRACE***)* Hey there, cutie.

(**GRACE** *exits to the bathroom.*)

BRUCE. How did you get in here?

MARLO. Own the place, remember?

BRUCE. I changed the locks.

(**MARLO** *shrugs.*)

BRUCE. You're supposed to be out of town.

MARLO. And you're supposed to be at the factory. And, uh, what was it? Married?

BRUCE. What are you doing here?

MARLO. Take it easy. I ain't here to judge. *(re:* **GRACE***)* Nice piece.

BRUCE. Thanks. She's not, by the way. A lesbian.

MARLO. I got that.

BRUCE. What are you doing here?

MARLO. I need the number of that lawyer. The one that did Dad's will.

BRUCE. What happened now?

MARLO. Hey, the 'me not judging' goes two ways, shithead. It's just a traffic ticket.

BRUCE. You don't need a lawyer for a traffic ticket. You got money. Pay it.

MARLO. That'd be all well and good, but they want a little more than money. It's my third time.

BRUCE. So, what? You're going to lose your license? How are you going to get to work?

MARLO. You think I give a shit about that? You only need a license if they pull you over. *(chuckles)* Fuckin' 'Mother-May-I', over here... That's not what I'm worried about. They're talkin' jail time.

BRUCE. So this is *more* than just a traffic ticket...

MARLO. *They're* calling it a D.U.I. But that's them. I gave the cop lip, so he went an' made up the charge. Breathalyzer didn't even move.

BRUCE. They can't just go and make up a charge. How much did you have?

MARLO. Not a single drop.

BRUCE. Marlo...

MARLO. Swear on the factory. Smell my breath if you wanna.

(**BRUCE** *goes over to inspect.* **MARLO** *breathes heavily out into his face.*)

MARLO. *(with his mouth still wide open as* **BRUCE** *inspects)* See?

BRUCE. *(sniffing)* What is that?

MARLO. Nothing!

BRUCE. It smells like shoe polish.

MARLO. You don't smell nothing so you gotta make up 'shoe polish'? You really fucking hate me, don't you, Bruce?

BRUCE. There's something there. What is that, paint?

MARLO. It's nothing.

BRUCE. Drugs?

MARLO. Fuck off. *(pause)* I... I had some of the feed stuff with the guys, but it's not fucking drugs.

BRUCE. Feed stuff?

MARLO. For the horses.

BRUCE. The horse steroids? You got high on horse steroids?

MARLO. It's not exactly a high, it's more like a—

BRUCE. How do you even...what, do you snort it?

(**MARLO** *shrugs*)

And you *drove*? This is just—

MARLO. Gimme a break.

BRUCE. Give you a break? I'm working my ass off trying to sell this place and you're off sniffing horse steroids and I'm supposed to give *you* a break?

MARLO. You need to give that up and keep it going like it is. That's the way Dad woulda wanted it.

BRUCE. Well, Dad was an idiot. And so are you if you want to spend the rest of your life working in that hellhole.

MARLO. You know, so far I've been nice enough not to say where I know that girl from.

BRUCE. Who?

MARLO. "*Who?*"

BRUCE. She works at Stroudy's. So what?

MARLO. You know what.

BRUCE. Whatever it is, it's between me and Carol. You don't have to—

MARLO. I don't give shitfuck about you an' Carol. That's Spoza's *wife*, man. His fucking wife! Is this why you switched him to nights? How long has this been going on?

BRUCE. About a year?

MARLO. He's my best friend, Bruce.

BRUCE. So?

MARLO. So, it's gonna be pretty hard facing him now that I know this.

BRUCE. Okay. What do you want?

MARLO. I don't want shit. You're just putting me in a tough spot. That's all.

BRUCE. I'm sorry about—

MARLO. I do need some money, though. Not because— Davey bailed me out and I hafta pay him back.

BRUCE. So *that's* why you broke in.

MARLO. Hey, you still owe me five grand.

BRUCE. How much do you need?

MARLO. Six hundred.

BRUCE. *(takes money from his wallet)* You're sure you're not going say anything, right?

MARLO. We're fucking brothers, man...

BRUCE. Okay.

(**BRUCE** *hands him the money.*)

MARLO. Fuckin' *brothers* man...

BRUCE. And as for the lawyer, there's a guy from my fraternity who owes me a favour. I'll get you his number.

MARLO. I don't need any of your prissy college pals bailing me out. I just want a normal lawyer.

BRUCE. All lawyers go to college.

MARLO. *(disappointed)* Oh.

(**BRUCE** *exits.* **MARLO** *walks over to the dresser and opens the drawer.*)

MARLO. Whoa. *(pulls out a handgun)* This yours?

BRUCE. *(offstage)* What?

(**BRUCE** *re-enters.*)

MARLO. *(pointing at* **BRUCE***)* Freeze, motherfucker!

BRUCE. Be careful! That's loaded.

MARLO. I can feel it. What is this, a forty-four? Lightweight?

BRUCE. I don't know.

MARLO. Stupid gun to have. 'Specially if you aren't smart enough to know what it is.

BRUCE. I bought it to go to that range you were talking about.

MARLO. How come I've never seen you there?

BRUCE. I only went once. I...didn't realize you could rent them, so I went out and bought one.

MARLO. I'd get rid of this if I were you.

BRUCE. *(sarcastic)* Oh, would you be willing to take it off my hands?

MARLO. Nah-uh. You know what I'm like when I hit the sauce. Last thing I need. *(adjusts gun)* Should probably keep the safety on.

(**MARLO** *puts the gun back in the drawer.* **GRACE** *exits from the bathroom, now wearing her Stroudy's uniform.*)

MARLO. Gotta say...kinda liked what you were wearing before.

GRACE. Charming.

MARLO. Yeah?

GRACE. Look, I heard about your DUI and I know a lawyer who'd be perfect. One of our cooks used him a while back and the guy's like...a *genius*. Pretty much all he handles.

MARLO. Even better.

BRUCE. That's nice, Grace, but my guy's one of the top criminal lawyers in the city.

GRACE. He's a *criminal* lawyer? Oh...

MARLO. No good?

GRACE. What are they going to think when the guy you hired to *represent* you deals only with criminals?

MARLO. Oh...

BRUCE. That's not how it—

GRACE. No, what *you* need is just a general, all-around lawyer. Someone local. Trustworthy. And that's what Sam is. He's even a member of the *bar association*.

MARLO. Whoa.

BRUCE. You *have* to be a member of the bar asso—

GRACE. And he's super cheap.

MARLO. No offense, Bruce, but I'm gonna go with the pretty face on this one.

GRACE. Come by Stroudy's tomorrow and I'll give you his card.

MARLO. Alright, I'm gonna leave you lovebirds to it. *(to* **BRUCE***)* And hey, thanks for the cash!

BRUCE. My pleasure.

*(***MARLO*** exits.)*

BRUCE. What was that?

GRACE. What?

BRUCE. This crap about an 'all around lawyer'? Criminal's *exactly* what he needs.

GRACE. I know.

BRUCE. You do?

GRACE. Sam Gilcrest is a total ambulance chaser. The judges *hate* him.

BRUCE. Then why would you—

GRACE. You said you need Marlo out of the way if you're ever gonna sell this place.

BRUCE. We can't do that...

GRACE. I thought you said you were serious about this?

BRUCE. I am, but...he's my brother.

GRACE. And he's *guilty*. You smelt his breath.

BRUCE. I did, but—

GRACE. You're not the one who made him drive loaded.

BRUCE. I can't just tell him to go to a lawyer that I know is—

GRACE. You're not. I am. In fact, you tried to help him. Right?

BRUCE. I guess.

GRACE. So it's not your fault if he didn't take your advice. Is it?

(Pause.)

BRUCE. I guess...it is up to him...

GRACE. Exactly. It's all up to him.

(Blackout.)

Scene Seven

(Present Day.)

(The breakroom. **MARLO** *is cleaning up the poker chips.* **BRUCE** *enters from the bathroom door, drying his hands with a paper towel.* **MARLO** *hands him a stack of bills.)*

MARLO. Here. We'll call it a friendly game.

BRUCE. I don't want your sympathy.

MARLO. It's not fucking sympathy. I just don't wanna play for keeps.

BRUCE. I'm not going to—

MARLO. I won, didn't I? That means I get to say what's what.

BRUCE. *(taking the money)* I woulda kept yours...

MARLO. Well, that's you.

*(***MARLO** *begins to clear the poker table.)*

MARLO. You talked to her yet?

BRUCE. Who?

MARLO. Your, uh... Grace.

BRUCE. Not since that last time at Stroudy's. I thought of going up to her after the service, but it seemed...

MARLO. Right.

BRUCE. Best not to do anything until we know what's going on. If there's a lesson to be learned here, it's definitely that.

MARLO. Is that some kinda dig?

BRUCE. What? No. I was just—

MARLO. Look, *you* said it was only him that was gonna be there. You didn't say anything about Spoza.

BRUCE. It wasn't a dig. And I didn't know either.

MARLO. "Wasn't a dig..." You *said*...you *fucking* said, alright? "He's the *only* one working, just go up there, press the fucking button. Get out." That's it. *That's* what you said.

BRUCE. Yes, but—

MARLO. *Is* that what you said?

BRUCE. Yes.

MARLO. Then it's on your fucking head. All of it.

BRUCE. Fine.

MARLO. Not me. You.

BRUCE. Well you *did* press the button.

MARLO. And who got me to do it, huh? Nah-uh. The way I see it, I'm just another button that got pushed. You pushed me, I pushed it. Weren't for you, none a' this woulda gone down. *None* of it.

BRUCE. If you say so.

MARLO. If you didn't try an' move this place behind my back... If you didn't do that—

BRUCE. There's nothing we can do about it now. It's over.

MARLO. How's it over? All these fines you got us paying, these *loans* we hadda take out. What? They just go *away* with Spoza?

BRUCE. No. But that's because it wasn't *him* that was supposed to—

MARLO. You should've covered *all* of 'em. That's what you made it sound like.

BRUCE. I didn't say that.

MARLO. You said four hundred thousand, right?

BRUCE. If we insured him. *If.*

MARLO. Well, you shoulda.

BRUCE. With all the extra money we have lying around?

MARLO. And whose fault is that?

BRUCE. *(grabs phone)* This isn't helping.

MARLO. Who you calling?

BRUCE. Eddle.

MARLO. He just called. Says we're not going to see any of it.

BRUCE. Figures...

MARLO. I told him to check into some of that worker's comp shit.

BRUCE. That's for the workers.

MARLO. We work.

BRUCE. We *employ*.

MARLO. Still work.

BRUCE. They're not going to help us.

MARLO. So what? A guy dies on our floor and we're not even gonna make a cent? How fucked is that?

BRUCE. I know.

MARLO. You shoulda put it on Spoza instead…

BRUCE. And then what? Send you out there all the same, thinking you're there to kill Davey?

MARLO. Yeah, laugh it up. You know it shoulda been him.

BRUCE. And what would happen when the police find out that I've been seeing Grace?

MARLO. Well, that could still happen, now, couldn't it?

BRUCE. Which is why it's good that we're not making money off her husband's death.

MARLO. Explain it all you want, that's who I woulda picked.

BRUCE. Isn't he your friend? Like, your *best* friend?

MARLO. He *were* my best friend. *Were.*

BRUCE. And now?

MARLO. He's dead.

BRUCE. But you would have gone ahead and killed him?

MARLO. Did anyways. Fuck does it matter now? Look, we still got Davey covered. Maybe we can do something with that.

BRUCE. We can't.

MARLO. It's a lot of money, Bruce. Money we're gonna need.

BRUCE. The police think he did it. We get rid of him, they're just going to look for someone new.

MARLO. Make it look like it's a problem with the machine, then. Starts on its own or something. That way we got excuses for both.

BRUCE. And what happens when they check and see nothing's wrong? They'll look at the guys cashing in.

MARLO. Stuff like that happens all the time! *(pointing to the toaster)* Here: you threw this toaster out last week 'cause it was broke, right? Well, I tried it in this morning and it works great. They come down on us we can just tell them about that.

BRUCE. About the toaster?

MARLO. Sure! It's proof something can break and go back to normal. I mean, it burns the toast a little, but other than that...

BRUCE. I threw it out *because* it burns the toast. That's how it's broken!

MARLO. Oh. *(beat)* We just won't tell them that part.

BRUCE. I'll figure something out.

MARLO. Like you figured out how to sell this place?

BRUCE. I said I was sor—

MARLO. *(suddenly irate)* You know what? *Forget* your girl sending me away with that piece of shit lawyer—

BRUCE. We *thought* he was good.

MARLO. — and forget you trying to unload this place behind my back. That's not the problem. The problem is that you're a *loser*, Bruce. That's right. Behind all that business card bullshit, it turns out you don't know shit about fuck. Oh, you *think* you do, but if you had any idea—any fucking idea how this place is supposed to go—

BRUCE. Okay...

MARLO. *NO*. Everyone on that floor knows Wilf Tricker's the only inspector that's gonna give this place a pass. *Everyone*. And here you are, calling in some cunt from the *government?* The fuck were you thinking? Why'd you think I was telling everyone how shitty this place is? 'Cause I enjoy your *company*? No, it's so they'd know better than to bring in an inspector. Bet that was your idea too, wasn't it?

BRUCE. No one told me.

MARLO. If you came an' visited me once, if you *told me* what you were up to, none of us would be in this mess. Two hundred grand in renos?

BRUCE. Okay...

MARLO. *(beat)* Dad was right to want you outta the will.

(A long pause.)

BRUCE. That's bullshit. He gave you just as much as me.

MARLO. Only 'cause Mom made him promise. And you can bet he wasn't happy about that. Even talked about going back and changing it after she kicked. But he couldn't break a promise. 'Gotta make way for the one who made good'. *(snorts)* Yeah, you really made good, didn't cha? The *probable* son returns...

*(A long pause. **DAVEY** enters, carrying his backpack and whistling a tune.)*

BRUCE. Get out.

DAVEY. I'm on my break.

BRUCE. We're having a meeting.

MARLO. *(to **DAVEY**)* Ah... don't worry about him. We're just about done. Have yourself some toast.

DAVEY. You fixed it?

MARLO. I got a gift...

*(**DAVEY** grabs two slices of bread from the counter and puts them in the toaster. He sits.)*

MARLO. Almost done?

DAVEY. 'Bout halfway.

BRUCE. Sure seem to be taking your time...

DAVEY. I gotta. On account'a the blood an' all. Everything's gotta get wiped with the alcohol twice. Floor, sides, all of it.

MARLO. What's this I hear about you getting a visit from the cops this morning?

DAVEY. Oh, yeah. They came to my house. Like eight a.m. or something. You believe that?

MARLO. Pigs...

DAVEY. I know, right? They drove me down to the station and started asking me all kindsa shit.

MARLO. You tell 'em to piss off? That's what I woulda done if I was you.

DAVEY. Well, if you was me, they'd have you as a suspect.

MARLO. So? You got nothing to hide.

DAVEY. I know.

MARLO. Heck, the only thing I'd worry about is what Spoza's girl is thinking 'bout all this. Cops going around calling you a *suspect*? Thing like that could ruin your *shot*. Soon as you finish here you oughta go over an' clear the air. Make sure she don't get any ideas.

BRUCE. He doesn't have a *shot*.

MARLO. Course he does! You shoulda seen her checking out that picture book of his. What was it, tattoos?

DAVEY. Yeah.

MARLO. Maybe you could give her one of those. Like a romantic thing. Beats flowers.

DAVEY. You think?

MARLO. Sure! Chicks dig creative shit. Gets their guard down. Do something a little fruity and then *BAM!* *(grabs crotch)* Hit 'em with it. Half the times I've gotten laid it's *right* after karaoke. Best way to go about it. You got that book on you?

DAVEY. *(opens his backpack)* Right here.

(**DAVEY** *hands him his sketchbook.* **MARLO** *looks through it.*)

MARLO. These aren't bad, Davey. Might have to ask you to give me one.

DAVEY. Oh sure. I'd love to try it on someone for real.

MARLO. You never done it?

DAVEY. Not on a person. I've done a bunch on my dog, though...

BRUCE. You tattooed your *dog*? This kid...

DAVEY. It's not like it's mean or nothing. I put him out the whole time and I even let him pick which one he wants. *(to MARLO)* I line all the pictures on the floor an' give him the one he stares at the longest.

MARLO. And it looks good?

DAVEY. Oh yeah. Especially now. There's a couple bad ones from back when I started, but I just let the hair grow over, no problem.

MARLO. *(re: book)* Hey, how about this one? I could have it up front. Like, pointing to my dick and shit.

DAVEY. Oh, you don't want that. That's a tramp stamp.

BRUCE. If the shoe fits...

MARLO. Ha ha, fucker. *(hands the book to BRUCE)* Here. See if anything calls to you.

DAVEY. Maybe all three of us could get the same one. Like a way to remember Spoza.

MARLO. There's an idea! Waddya say, Bruce?

BRUCE. I wouldn't wear any of these on a *shirt*.

MARLO. Ah, Bruce...

BRUCE. If I were you, I'd keep practicing your scrubbing.

(Pause. DAVEY starts whimpering.)

MARLO. Hey, hey. Why don't you back off? Davey here is an *artist*. Don't let 'im get to you, buddy. He's just jealous you gotta shot with a nice girl and he hasta commute for his pussy.

BRUCE. Fuck you.

DAVEY. You... you really think I have a shot?

MARLO. Sure, why not?

BRUCE. He killed her husband. How's that for 'why not'?

DAVEY. That's not true.

BRUCE. As far as she knows, it is.

MARLO. Alright, take it easy... Both of us know you had nothin' to do with it. It was probably just something with the equipment.

DAVEY. You think?

MARLO. Sure.

DAVEY. Works fine now, though...

MARLO. Yeah, but that's 'cause it fixed itself. Those things out there? They're like us. Get worked too hard, they start messin' up. All it needed was a little sleep. You'd buy that, wouldn't you?

DAVEY. Makes sense.

MARLO. *(to BRUCE)* See? It makes *sense*.

(**DAVEY** *removes his bread from the toaster.*)

DAVEY. Aw. It's all burnt...

MARLO. Nah, it's still good. Just scrape off the ugly.

(**MARLO** *hands* **DAVEY** *a plastic knife.* **DAVEY** *walks over to the garbage can and begins to scrape off the burnt toast.*)

DAVEY. Maybe I shouldn't go back down there.

BRUCE. You trying to get out of work?

DAVEY. No, but if—

BRUCE. Because I have the names of twenty guys who'd be more than happy to take your place.

DAVEY. It's just...if it could happen to Spoza for no reason...

BRUCE. *If* it happened for no reason.

DAVEY. I swear I didn't—

MARLO. Bruce... *(to* **DAVEY***)* Tell you what. *(walks over to switchbox)* We'll turn the power off from in here. That way, nothing can happen.

(**MARLO** *flips a switch. The lighting goes off on the factory floor.*)

MARLO. There. You're safe. *(hands him a flashlight)* Now, get out there. We got a meeting to finish.

DAVEY. But...

BRUCE. What?

DAVEY. It's dark.

MARLO. *(re: flashlight)* That's what this is for.

DAVEY. Yeah, but...

BRUCE. What?

DAVEY. Nothing. *(begins to leave)* I'll, uh, be down on the floor if you need me.

BRUCE. And don't you go off trying to sneak smokes! We can hear when you're working.

DAVEY. I know.

*(***DAVEY** *hesitates, grabs his backpack and exits. A sheet of paper falls from his back pocket as he exits.)*

BRUCE. I see what you're trying to do there with the Grace thing.

MARLO. I'm not trying anything. He's going after her on his own. But if you wanna *do something* about it...

BRUCE. It's too risky.

MARLO. Shoulda thought a' that before this started.

*(***MARLO** *notices the sheet of paper on the floor. He picks it up and begins to read it.)*

MARLO. Huh.

BRUCE. What?

MARLO. You know, Eddle said something else when he called. That girlfriend of yours?

BRUCE. She's not my girlfriend.

MARLO. Whatever she is, she's trying to sue us for a quarter mill. You believe that? 'Unsafe working conditions'.

BRUCE. Hard to argue with that.

MARLO. That all you got to say?

BRUCE. We're going to have to file for bankruptcy anyways. It's just another thing on the pile.

MARLO. I'm not losing the factory. Not because of this.

*(***MARLO** *begins to leave.)*

BRUCE. Where are you going?

MARLO. Gonna pick up some things.

BRUCE. What things?

MARLO. *Things.* You think you're the only one with ideas around here? *(hands him the sheet)* You might wanna give that a look-see.

BRUCE. What is it?

MARLO. Fell outta Davey's pocket. Some kinda speech.

BRUCE. So?

MARLO. Check out the big note up top.

BRUCE. *(reading)* "Don't mention you got a thing for Grace. They'll think that's why you killed Spoza."

MARLO. Ah?

BRUCE. We already knew he had a thing for Grace. So what?

MARLO. Doesn't it sound like he's got something to hide? Like maybe he *did something* to Spoza?

BRUCE. But he didn't.

MARLO. Yeah, but *they* don't know that. Don't you get it, Bruce? We don't have to fake another accident. All we gotta do is make sure this fucker *disappears.*

*(**MARLO** exits. **BRUCE** goes back to his crossword puzzle. Lights out.)*

End of Act I

ACT II

Scene One

(TITLE: FOUR MONTHS EARLIER.)

(Stroudy's Pub and Grill. **DAVEY** *is seated at the bar,* **GRACE** *is standing behind it. She's preparing a drink. She hands it to him.)*

GRACE. Comes to four.

DAVEY. *(he hands her a ten dollar bill)* Keep the change.

GRACE. This is a ten.

DAVEY. So?

GRACE. So, your tip is bigger than the bill.

DAVEY. In, uh, more ways than *one...*

GRACE. What?

DAVEY. It's a joke. Like a sex...er, uh...penis thing.

GRACE. You're saying your dick is bigger than the bill?

DAVEY. Yeah. It's one of those double wordies.

GRACE. The bill's *four.*

DAVEY. Yeah!

GRACE. I'd assume you're bigger than four.

DAVEY. Thank you.

GRACE. I'd assume *everyone's* bigger than four.

DAVEY. Well I said it was *bigger,* okay? It could be anything. Jeez, if I'd a known you'd make a thing of it, I woulda said it better. Measure exact and tip that much.

GRACE. Do you need anything else?

DAVEY. *(defeated)* No...

*(***GRACE*** exits.* **DAVEY** *holds out his fingers to approximate one inch. He does the same with his other*

hand, and puts them together. He begins stacking them on top of each, while attempting to count. **BRUCE** *sits down next to him.*)

DAVEY. Hey, Mr. Cafferty! *(beat)* So, uh, me an' Spoza are gonna go see Marlo tomorrow night... Probably the last time we'll get down there before they let him out. You wanna come?

BRUCE. I'll pass.

DAVEY. I think he'd really like it if you did.

BRUCE. Has he said anything about me?

DAVEY. He's kinda pissed about the repainting. Says it's a waste since it's only us can see it.

BRUCE. Why'd you tell him about that?

DAVEY. He wants to know what's going on. I think he misses the place.

(**GRACE** *re-enters. She sees* **BRUCE** *and hovers in the background*)

BRUCE. When are you leaving?

DAVEY. Right after we get off.

BRUCE. How 'bout I let you both pull a half shift tomorrow? That way you can make it there before sundown.

DAVEY. You'd do that?

BRUCE. Only if you promise to knock off right now. If you're only going to do half, I want you at full.

DAVEY. Sure thing. *(downs drink)* Take 'er easy.

(**DAVEY** *exits.* **GRACE** *enters.*)

GRACE. Well?

BRUCE. What?

GRACE. I'm waiting to hear your excuse.

BRUCE. *My* excuse?

GRACE. You have any idea how hard it was to get Saint Patrick's Day off? That's our biggest weekend. I coulda made four hundred, easy.

BRUCE. You're right.

(**BRUCE** *takes out his wallet and begins to pull out some bills.*)

GRACE. What are you doing?

BRUCE. Making up the difference.

GRACE. Now you're going to pay me off like some whore?

BRUCE. No. If anything it's the opposite. The money's 'cause we didn't—

GRACE. Fuck you.

BRUCE. *(places the money in the tip jar)* Fine. Split it with the others, if it makes you happier.

GRACE. You're a real prick, you know that?

(Pause.)

BRUCE. You called my *house*.

GRACE. I thought you got into an accident or something! I didn't think you'd be so inconsiderate as to not even call.

BRUCE. We're lucky it was me that answered.

GRACE. *You're* lucky. Why did you go back?

BRUCE. I had to meet with my lawyer. We, um…we found a buyer for the factory.

GRACE. That's great.

BRUCE. Yeah, the building inspector's coming tomorrow and after that it's pretty much a done deal.

GRACE. So did you tell her?

BRUCE. Tell her what?

GRACE. About us.

BRUCE. *(pause)* Look, I've been giving this a lot of thought and the timing right now isn't—

GRACE. I don't believe this.

BRUCE. We're already underselling because of the economy and then there's Marlo's half—

GRACE. I don't care about—   **BRUCE.** — not to mention the child support…

GRACE. I don't *care* about the money.

BRUCE. It's not like we're walking away with nothing. You still have Gary and—

GRACE. That's worse than nothing.

BRUCE. Kid's going to be a lawyer someday. Trust me, you'll be way better off down the line.

GRACE. He dropped out. Thinks he's gonna make it with his band.

BRUCE. Well, hey, maybe he can. That show they did here? That was really something.

GRACE. You're really trying to make this easy on yourself, aren't you?

BRUCE. So you hit a rough spot... It's nothing that can't be—

GRACE. *(almost inaudible)* He hits me.

BRUCE. He does not *hate* you.

GRACE. HITS me. You moron. He *hits* me. *(beat)* Yeah. You got an answer for that one? *(pause)* Course you already knew that, didn't you?

BRUCE. Grace, If I had any idea...

GRACE. You'd what? What would you do?

BRUCE. *(beat)* What...would you *want* me to do?

(Pause.)

GRACE. You *did* get it. That night I told you that he and the band were getting back together? That he was the only one I'd been with besides you? You *knew* what that meant. I wanted to think it was 'cause you were thick, but you figured it out. You just didn't want to be bothered.

BRUCE. Grace...

GRACE. You wanna know the real reason I was at those meetings? Gary found a phone number in my apron. I get them every other night, but I always make sure to throw them out. This one time I forgot. Maybe I didn't, I dunno. But, he found it and things went way worse than usual. Broke three ribs. Even had me bring his motorcycle helmet to emergency so the doctors wouldn't get suspicious. After that, he kept going on about how I was this huge slut that needed to get fixed. "Get fixed." That's what he called it. Threatened to kill me if I didn't. So I'd go to these meetings and sit there, all the time hoping for some way out. For some dumb reason you had me convinced it could be you.

BRUCE. I really wanted it to work, Grace. But there's all these complications, and my family...

GRACE. It's the easier one to go with. I get it.

BRUCE. I love them.

GRACE. Oh, so you *can* say it. *(pause)* This was just a dumb fling to you, wasn't it?

BRUCE. If I had any idea at the time—

GRACE. "If I had any idea". You and your bullshit words. No, the only way to tell with people is by what they do. Their actions. And you know what yours tell me, Bruce? You really *are* a faggot. *(pause)* Now get the fuck out of my bar.

*(**BRUCE** exits. **GRACE** pulls the bills from the tip jar and stuffs them in her apron pocket. Lights out.)*

Scene Two

(Present day.)

(Split stage. The break room is exactly the same as before. **BRUCE** *is sitting at the table on the phone. To the right of the stage is the interior of* **GRACE***'s trailer.* **GRACE** *sits in a chair, staring at a TV set with a blue VCR screen. A phone behind her rings. After the fifth ring, an answering machine picks up.)*

GRACE'S VOICE. *(unenthused)* You've reached the offices of the Solid Gold Excellence Talent Agency, exclusive representatives for the hit up-and-coming band, 'Acid Snatch'. If you'd like to book them or are one of the *many* major record labels that have expressed interest in signing them, please leave your message at the...*shriek.*

(A loud male scream is heard over the answering machine, followed by a beep.)

BRUCE. Grace. It's me. We really need to talk. (**GRACE** *sighs, gets up and walks towards the phone.)* I know you're there... *(beat)* Look, if you're not going to pick up, I'm just gonna have to keep calling back until—

*(***GRACE*** pulls the phone cord from the wall. Lights out on* **BRUCE***. A knock at the door.* **GRACE** *answers. It's* **DAVEY***. He's wearing his suit and carrying his backpack.)*

GRACE. What are you doing here?

DAVEY. Can I come in? I just wanted to talk to you about—

GRACE. Kinda want to be on my own right now.

DAVEY. I won't be too long, it's just...it's about Spo—your husband. Well, I guess he's not your husband anymore, but—

GRACE. What do you want?

DAVEY. I didn't kill him.

GRACE. *(starting to close the door)* Okay.

DAVEY. It's just...some people think it was me that did it. I was the only one there when it happened, so—

GRACE. That was you?

DAVEY. That's the thing! I wasn't even—I went to the Sev to get some smokes and everything was good when I left, but when I came back he was...

(**DAVEY** *whines nervously.*)

GRACE. Dead?

DAVEY. I just didn't want to say it in case you—

GRACE. I'm not in denial. I know he's dead.

DAVEY. I brought you these.

(**DAVEY** *pulls out a pack of cigarettes.*)

GRACE. I don't smoke cloves.

DAVEY. No, it's not–This is my proof.

GRACE. Your *proof?*

DAVEY. That I didn't do it. They're Djarums, see? The only place that sells them is that one way out by the highway. That's why I was gone so long. It's like a half hour drive.

GRACE. Where's the receipt?

DAVEY. Why would I get a receipt?

GRACE. If you want this to be proof, you're gonna need a receipt. No one's gonna believe you on just this.

DAVEY. No one?

GRACE. Not me, anyway.

DAVEY. You gotta believe me. I was gone the whole hour.

GRACE. So if you were there, you would've stopped it?

DAVEY. Absolutely.

GRACE. And you *were* supposed to be there, right?

DAVEY. Yeah...

GRACE. So then it kind of is your fault.

DAVEY. Oh no. It *is.*

GRACE. There ya go.

(GRACE closes the door on him. A knock on the door. **GRACE** *re-opens the door.* **DAVEY** *has tears streaming down his face.)*

GRACE. Christ.

DAVEY. I am...so...so...*(sniffs)* so-rry!

*(**DAVEY** continues to bawl uncontrollably.)*

GRACE. Okay now. Stop crying. Just...come inside and we'll—

DAVEY. I'm a *killer*!

GRACE. You're not a—Keep it down. You're not a—I was just fucking with you.

DAVEY. It should have been *me* in there—

GRACE. Alright...

DAVEY. I mean, if I'da known...

GRACE. You couldn't have.

DAVEY. I should've...

GRACE. Let me get you some Kleenex.

*(**GRACE** exits the room. **DAVEY** finishes crying and pulls a tattoo gun from his backpack. He begins to prep it.)*

DAVEY. Hey, Grace?

GRACE. *(offstage)* Yeah?

DAVEY. What was Spoza's favorite thing?

GRACE. *(offstage)* What?

DAVEY. What did he like most? I didn't really know him that well.

GRACE. *(offstage)* I don't know. He liked to play the drums...

DAVEY. Is there a symbol for that? Like a Chinese one?

*(**GRACE** re-enters. She sits down next to him and hands him the Kleenex.)*

GRACE. I don't know Chinese.

DAVEY. But you're all—

GRACE. I'm from here. Just like you.

DAVEY. What about your parents?

GRACE. My dad's white, my mom's from Thailand.

DAVEY. That's like a *kind* of Chinese, isn't it?

GRACE. No.

DAVEY. I guess I could try drawing it for real… *(visualizing it in his mind)* Drums. *(turns the tattoo gun on)* Do you want the left or the right?

GRACE. What are you doing?

DAVEY. Everyone at work's getting a tattoo to remember him by. I'm gonna let you have the first.

GRACE. Please get that away from me.

DAVEY. *(turns off gun)* You don't have to worry. I've got loadsa practice. I've never done drums, though. Did he like bacon? I'm real good at drawing bacon.

GRACE. I'm gonna pass.

(Pause.)

DAVEY. I, uh, noticed you didn't cry at the funeral…

GRACE. You more than made up for that.

DAVEY. I'm not trying to be mean or anything. It was just kinda brave, is all. Were you tryin' to think of other things? Because I've tried that and it never seems to work.

GRACE. I just couldn't. Believe me, I wanted to. It's kind of expected.

DAVEY. Probably hasn't hit you yet. I think once you start thinking about the good times…

GRACE. *(gestures towards the TV)* I just watched our wedding tape.

DAVEY. Did that work?

GRACE. No. I taped over it, actually.

DAVEY. Why?

GRACE. I didn't want it around trying to convince me we were something we weren't. We didn't exactly have the best relationship.

DAVEY. Oh.

GRACE. I guess I just wanted to get away from my dad so badly that I ended up marrying somebody just like him.

DAVEY. I could never marry my dad.

GRACE. I guess it doesn't matter now. Maybe I'll get some money from it and finally be able to leave this shithole. Move to the city or something.

DAVEY. You *are* brave.

GRACE. It's not really brave when there's nothing holding you back.

DAVEY. I always wished I could do something like that. *(re: tattoo gun)* Like go off an' do this for a living.

GRACE. Why don't you?

DAVEY. I just made assistant super and the guys are starting to treat me nicer. I don't wanna hafta start over. Plus I got Baby to think of.

GRACE. You have a kid?

DAVEY. No, Baby's my dog. Eats as much as one though. That's the other nice thing 'bout working there. They give me a discount on feed. It's for horses, but he loves it. It wouldn't be fair goin' off tryin' to be an artist when I got him counting on me.

GRACE. I thought you just wanted to do tattoos.

DAVEY. It's called a tattoo *artist. (beat)* I should get going.

GRACE. You can stay if you want.

DAVEY. I'd like to, but I'm actually suppose'ta be at work right now. *(looks at watch)* I only got about fifteen minutes before I have to be back. You don't still have my number, do you?

GRACE. I lost it. I actually thought about calling, but me and Gary were trying to work things out and—

DAVEY. I would have never asked if I knew you two were—

GRACE. I know.

DAVEY. Do you think it'd be okay if you didn't say anything about that to the police? I'm just worried that if they thought I had a thing for you it might be a reason to, y'know...*do something* to Spoza.

GRACE. You think so?

DAVEY. Well, it's a pretty good reason.

GRACE. *(beat)* Yeah. I guess it is.

DAVEY. Oh no. I shouldn't have said anything. Look, you're nice an' all but I could never–

GRACE. What? No, I didn't mean... *(beat)* I'm just fucking with you again.

DAVEY. Oh. Heh. That's...funny.

GRACE. You be safe out there, okay?

DAVEY. Will do. 'Night, Grace.

GRACE. Goodnight, Davey.

*(**DAVEY** nods and exits. **GRACE** goes over to the TV and turns it off. Lights out.)*

Scene Three

(TITLE: FIVE DAYS EARLIER)

(Stroudy's restaurant. **DAVEY** *and* **MARLO** *are seated at a table looking at* **DAVEY***'s sketchbook.* **GRACE** *is standing.)*

GRACE. Your little friend's pretty talented.

DAVEY. Not little…

MARLO. Ah, look at him stick up for himself! Ain't that cute. *(to* **GRACE***)* Listen, he's just about ready to settle up here, but I'm gonna stay. You mind splitting the bill?

GRACE. No problem.

*(***GRACE** *exits.)*

DAVEY. I'm working the night shift tomorrow. I could stay a bit longer.

MARLO. If it was up to me, I'd say yes, but Bruce and I are gonna have a meeting.

DAVEY. Well, since I'm a super now—

MARLO. *Assistant* super. This is a bosses only thing.

DAVEY. Oh.

*(***GRACE** *returns with the check holder.)*

GRACE. Thirteen even.

DAVEY. Alright, let me just… *(pulls out some bills)* Here you go.

GRACE. Thanks.

DAVEY. Hey, uh…check the tip. Go on, check it.

GRACE. Seven dollars.

DAVEY. Oh, wait. Here. *(hands her two quarters)* Seven-*fifty*. Heh?

*(***BRUCE** *enters.)*

GRACE. You must be very proud. *(to* **BRUCE***)* Bar's closed.

*(***GRACE** *exits.)*

MARLO. *(shouting to* **GRACE***)* Ah, come on...he just got here!
BRUCE. I'm fine.
MARLO. Well, I'm not!
DAVEY. See you tomorrow.
MARLO. Later.

(**DAVEY** *exits. Pause.*)

BRUCE. So. Are we on for tomorrow?
MARLO. No go.
BRUCE. What?
MARLO. Can't do it. Not right.
BRUCE. It's our only way out of this.
MARLO. I'm not looking to get out.
BRUCE. With all the debt we're taking you will be. One way or another.
MARLO. If it ends, it ends. Plenty of places like ours. I'll find something.
BRUCE. What? Another *feed mill?*
MARLO. It's what I'm good at.
BRUCE. Wouldn't you rather spend your life doing something you actually like?
MARLO. It's not that bad.
BRUCE. But that's *all* it is. Every generation—Okay, *every* generation has to improve on the last. Otherwise they fail. We owe it to ourselves...we owe it to *Dad* to go beyond what he did. Right now we're only doing half each. And pretty soon we won't even have that.
MARLO. He's a good kid.
BRUCE. Maybe. But look at him. World's not gonna change either way.
MARLO. If he's so dumb, why'd you make him super? Spoza's the one that deserved it.
BRUCE. You get more money from the insurance if they're higher up.
MARLO. How much?

BRUCE. Average guy on the floor can bring in four hundred thousand. A super is worth six.

MARLO. Huh.

BRUCE. Think of what you could do with that! You could get into business with something you *want*. Have your own bar...

MARLO. Don't...

BRUCE. There's that place on Tesler that just closed. You could buy it up! Get yourself one of those apartments upstairs. Have a cook send up all your meals, open bar... You could even start a *karaoke* night!

(Pause.)

MARLO. Karaoke, huh?

BRUCE. All you hafta do is push one button.

MARLO. Why can't you do it?

BRUCE. Because I'm the one who took out the policy. They'll look into me the most. You want this just as much as I do.

(Pause.)

MARLO. Y'know, when I was away, there was this guy who was in for killing three people.

BRUCE. This is just one. And we're not going to get caught.

MARLO. That's what he thought. Some guy that messed up his girl, one of those things that needed to be done, right?

BRUCE. Uh-huh.

MARLO. Only thing was, he didn't know the guy had roommates. They come home early and he ends up having to do two more. Good guys too, never hurt anyone. I ask why he didn't just run and you know what he said? He said killing's like lying. Once you start, you gotta keep going 'til it covers itself up. And that only happens if you're *lucky*.

BRUCE. Marlo. I *feel* lucky.

MARLO. I don't.

(Pause.)

BRUCE. Okay. Fair enough.

*(****BRUCE*** *starts to get up.)*

MARLO. What are you playin' at, "fair enough"?

BRUCE. If you don't want to be part of it, I'll find someone else. Policy's in my name. I was just going to cut you in 'cause we're family. Spoza doesn't care much for Davey, does he?

MARLO. And what if I say something?

BRUCE. You won't.

MARLO. Why not?

BRUCE. Because we're *brothers. (beat)* Don't look at me like that, you know how bad we're in.

MARLO. You got the best of both here. Why fuck it up? That Grace is one fine piece of—

BRUCE. It's over between us.

MARLO. Ah, I'm sorry to hear that. You were, uh…you were too good for her.

BRUCE. I'm the one who broke up with her.

MARLO. *Really?*

BRUCE. *Yes*, really.

MARLO. Huh. Well, you're both better off.

BRUCE. Not as long as she's with that asshole.

MARLO. That's my best friend you're talking about there.

BRUCE. Your best friend's a piece of shit.

MARLO. How do you figure?

BRUCE. Nevermind.

MARLO. No, you have something here. What is it?

BRUCE. It's personal.

MARLO. That's why I want to know!

BRUCE. Well…*apparently*, from time to time, Spoza would…

MARLO. What?

BRUCE. Hit her.

MARLO. *Hit* her?

BRUCE. Yeah...

MARLO. You sure about this?

BRUCE. She told me when we broke up.

MARLO. Maybe it was one of those woman things. Like, maybe she made it up to make you feel...*sorry* or something.

BRUCE. No. She's definitely not—I've seen the bruises. I...I just always figured her for clumsy.

MARLO. *(pause)* So...what are you going to *do* about it?

BRUCE. About...

MARLO. I mean, this guy's hitting your girl—

BRUCE. She's not my girl.

MARLO. She *was*. I can't believe you're still letting him work for us!

BRUCE. If I fire him it could...he might— I can't afford any unnecessary attention right now. Carol already has her suspicions and—

MARLO. Unbelievable.

BRUCE. What can I do?

MARLO. Well, fucking *something*, man. Jesus!

(GRACE returns to the table with a check holder. She avoids eye contact with BRUCE.)

GRACE. We're closing in five.

MARLO. Don't worry sweetheart, we're about to clear out.

(GRACE exits. BRUCE picks up the bill.)

BRUCE. So tomorrow...am I in this alone?

MARLO. You're gonna be doing this either way, huh?

BRUCE. Yes.

MARLO. Nothing I can do to change your mind?

BRUCE. 'Fraid not.

(Pause.)

MARLO. Alright. But I want half.

BRUCE. Okay. *(beat)* Now, it's just you and him tomorrow night. Call in sick and make sure no one sees you.

MARLO. I know how it's done.

BRUCE. *(getting up)* Course you do. And Marlo?

MARLO. Yeah?

BRUCE. Good luck.

    *(**BRUCE** exits. Lights out.)*

Scene Four

(Present day.)

(The break room. **DAVEY***'s whistling can be heard from the darkened floor below.* **BRUCE** *is at the table doing crosswords. He appears to be struggling for an answer and after a moment opens the book to the back page. As he does this, the sound of a truck can be heard.* **MARLO** *enters from the outside door, peeking his head into the door frame.* **BRUCE** *quickly closes his book, putting it aside.)*

MARLO. Where's Davey?

BRUCE. Down in the augers.

MARLO. Make sure he stays there.

*(***MARLO** *exits to the parking lot. After a moment, he returns carrying a plastic laundry basket. He drops it on the table.)*

BRUCE. What's this?

MARLO. Davey's.

*(***MARLO** *goes back out the door.* **BRUCE** *fishes through the basket. He pulls out some clothing, the gun for an old Nintendo system, and an issue of "Heavy Metal". The truck lights and engine noises stop.* **BRUCE** *walks over to the outside door.)*

BRUCE. What the ...

*(***MARLO** *enters, dragging the body of a preposterously large dog by its hind legs. It is wrapped with blue tarp and bungee cords.)*

BRUCE. Is that—

MARLO. Baby. Figured him for a poodle with a name like that! Must be something in the food, huh?

BRUCE. What happened?

MARLO. Went to clean out his place an' the fucker got up on me. Had no choice. 'Sides, makes no sense him taking off without his baby.

BRUCE. Taking off?

MARLO. Good thing I stopped by yours first. Thing woulda eaten me alive. *(kicks the dog)* Probably woulda fit, huh?

BRUCE. Why were you at my place?

*(**MARLO** pulls back his jacket, revealing the gun.)*

BRUCE. You *shot* this thing?

MARLO. Didn't die a' hunger.

BRUCE. Christ, Marlo...

MARLO. You're the one said we couldn't kill him by accident.

BRUCE. So we kill his dog instead?

MARLO. No, shithead. We make it look like he took off.

BRUCE. Again with the took off...

MARLO. Cops are lookin' into him and now we got that dumb letter saying how much he loves Grace? The second he stops showing up places they'll figure he fled. An' then we'll get the money. Done deal.

BRUCE. How do we 'get' the money?

MARLO. He's dead.

BRUCE. But they don't know he's dead. They'll think he ran off.

MARLO. But he *is* dead.

BRUCE. How do they know that? *(pause)* Some plan.

MARLO. Fuck you! That's a thing, ain't it? After you been missing a while they just figure you for dead.

BRUCE. Yes. But it takes a while.

MARLO. Nah... I'm pretty sure it's only a couple weeks. Every time they do one of those searches that's when they give up. A couple weeks.

BRUCE. No...

MARLO. Why would they stop searching for you if you're still alive?

BRUCE. It's more than two weeks, I know that.

MARLO. Whatever it is, we'll just keep paying the bills off 'til we get what's ours. 'Sides, it's not like we got muchuva choice now. *(checks watch)* Kid's gonna be done in an hour and once he sees what we did to his dog—

BRUCE. *You* did.

MARLO. Well as soon as he sees this he'll figure things out pretty quick. *(beat)* Nah, the only thing to do now is the same we did to Spoza, 'cept we hide it afterwards.

BRUCE. Marlo, we can't...

MARLO. You read that speech. Money or no money, pretty soon he's going to say something that'll bring it all back to us.

BRUCE. He did mention the insurance.

MARLO. See?

BRUCE. I don't think he knows what it means.

MARLO. He wouldn't be down there if he did. But sooner or later someone's gonna figure it out. And that's *your* name on the policy, Bruce. I mean, I go away, it's just me. But you got a wife 'an kids...

(Pause.)

BRUCE. I know.

MARLO. It's just one more button we hafta push. One button.

BRUCE. *(beat)* Okay.

MARLO. Good man.

(A long pause.)

BRUCE. So are you going to...

MARLO. Me? Nah... This one's on you.

BRUCE. You're the one who wants it done.

MARLO. I didn't want any of this, brother.

BRUCE. I wouldn't even know how to...

MARLO. Just go out there an' press it. I'll help you clean up.

BRUCE. But...

MARLO. What?

BRUCE. You've already done it.

MARLO. Exactly why it should be you. How can I trust you if you're not gonna pull your end? *(pause)* Go on.

BRUCE. You need to—

MARLO. What?

BRUCE. *(points to power box)* You need to turn the power back on.

MARLO. That's a lightswitch, dummy. You really know fuck all about this place, don't you?

(**BRUCE** *climbs the ladder. He walks over to the control panel, hesitates and presses it. A loud buzzer rings, followed by the sound of rotating augers.* **BRUCE** *returns to the break room.*)

MARLO. That's a pretty big pair you got there.

BRUCE. Yeah.

MARLO. Good kid, but when it's us or him that doesn't really matter now, does it?

BRUCE. Mmm-hmm.

MARLO. Nothin' either of us coulda done.

BRUCE. Nope.

MARLO. Nothing at all.

(Pause.)

BRUCE. Marlo?

MARLO. Yeah?

BRUCE. Were the lights off when Spoza died?

MARLO. Course not.

BRUCE. Then how come you didn't see him?

MARLO. See who?

BRUCE. You have to look down to press that button. I mean, I couldn't see anything 'cause of the dark, but those are some bright fluorescents. Couldn't you tell it was Spoza?

MARLO. Yeah. I could tell.

BRUCE. You could?

MARLO. I'm not as big a fuck up as you think, Bruce. I went in thinking I'd have to do Davey, but when I got up 'an saw it was Spoza, I started thinkin'. I figured if I kill Davey, that's something that's gonna stick with me a long time. But knowing what Spoza did to Grace? Doing something like that didn't seem half as bad. At least not as bad as Davey. An' since you made it sound like we had both of 'em covered, I figured four hundred'd be enough.

BRUCE. I didn't *say* he was covered.

MARLO. So I heard wrong. That one's on me.

BRUCE. He was your best friend.

MARLO. *Were.* I guess I just didn't have it in me to kill a guy who did nothing wrong.

BRUCE. But...you made *me* do it.

MARLO. Only after you made me pop my cherry. It's not like I'm gonna let Spoza happen for nothing. *(pause, gestering towards the augers)* You can probably turn those off now.

BRUCE. You're sick.

MARLO. *(chuckling)* You might be right about that, brother. Might be right about that.

*(**BRUCE** climbs the ladder and presses the stop button. He climbs back down to the breakroom, grabs a Kleenex off the table and wipes his eyes.)*

MARLO. Ah...what's this? You kill him, suddenly you get his *powers?*

*(**BRUCE** attacks **MARLO**.)*

MARLO. The fuck?

BRUCE. Do you realize what you've done here? Two people are dead 'cause of you. You and your fucking ideas.

MARLO. Me? You're the one that wanted it to—

BRUCE. *One.* I only wanted one.

(**BRUCE** *begins to choke* **MARLO**.)

MARLO. *(struggling to breathe)* I...didn't...want...*any*.

(*A loud clang can be heard coming from the auger floor.*)

BRUCE. What was that?

MARLO. What?

(**BRUCE** *lets go of* **MARLO**. *The sound repeats itself.*)

MARLO. That's just the floor settling. It happens all the—

(*A knock comes from the outside door.* **MARLO** *grabs the gun from the table and moves away from the door's sightline.*)

MARLO. Get it.

(**BRUCE** *walks over to the door and opens it slightly.*)

BRUCE. Oh, hi. *(turns to* **MARLO***)* It's Grace.

MARLO. *(hiding the gun behind his back)* Let her in.

BRUCE. I've been, uh, trying to get ahold of you all night.

GRACE. *(entering)* I know. Marlo.

MARLO. Nice to see ya, Grace. Real sorry to hear about your—

GRACE. What were you calling about?

BRUCE. Just wanted to check in. See how you were doi—

GRACE. You want me to drop the lawsuit. Isn't that it?

MARLO. It'd be nice...

BRUCE. *Marlo.* *(to* **GRACE***)* No, that wasn't—It's just we didn't get the chance to talk at the funeral and—

GRACE. Because I will.

MARLO. Now that's talking!

GRACE. I'd rather be paid up front if it's all the same.

MARLO. Hold on, now...

GRACE. I figure if I go through lawyers they'll just take half anyway. So let's just say two hundred and fifty thousand, up front.

MARLO. Why would we do something like that?

GRACE. Because if you *don't*, I'll tell the police what I know.

MARLO. And what's that?

GRACE. How about the fact that he was having an affair with me for over a year? You don't think they'll be able to do something with that? Because it's pretty obvious to me why he's dead. It was all just some plan to get me back, wasn't it?

MARLO. *(laughs)* Missy, you're way off. If anything, it's the opposite.

BRUCE. Marlo!

MARLO. *(pulls out gun)* Nothing to hide, Bruce. She's right. We're the ones that killed him.

GRACE. You did?

BRUCE. *He* did.

MARLO. Fine. *I* did. "My own little idea."

BRUCE. That's not what I wanted, Grace, honest. It wasn't supposed to be him.

MARLO. It was supposed to be Davey.

GRACE. Why would you want to kill Davey?

MARLO. Insurance. Coulda got six hundred thou, too. But then Brucie here let me in on a little secret and killing Spoza didn't seem like such a bad idea.

GRACE. Secret?

MARLO. Something to do with you.

GRACE. So that's what this was? Payback?

MARLO. You could say that.

GRACE. Because of that lawyer? *(to BRUCE)* Why'd you tell him about that?

BRUCE. That's not what he's—

MARLO. *Lawyer?* I was talking about Spoza hurting you.

GRACE. Oh.

MARLO. Yeah. I was talking about doing you a fucking *kindness*. What's this about a lawyer?

GRACE. Nothing.

MARLO. That asshat you hooked me up with! That was some kind of trick?

GRACE. No. Not at all. It wasn't—

MARLO. That shithead didn't know shit! You *knew* that?

GRACE. No. Everyone said he was great, I just thought...

MARLO. Mother-fucker! *(pointing gun towards BRUCE)* Were you in on this?

BRUCE. Hey, I told you to go with my guy.

MARLO. Bullshit. She figured you for telling me.

BRUCE. Okay. Yes, but I only found out after we broke up. Seriously, if I had any idea—

MARLO. *(moving towards him)* Well, that about does it for me...

BRUCE. Marlo...c'mon. We're brothers. Brothers. Do you really think I would go that far to sell a fucking factory? Sending my own brother to jail? Do you really think that's the kind of person I am?

MARLO. You knew! You fuckin' knew!

BRUCE. Just the night we broke up. And you know what? It's why we broke up. It's been eating away at me every since.

MARLO. Huh. *(to GRACE)* That true?

(**BRUCE** gestures at **GRACE** to "go along with it".)

BRUCE. Tell him.

GRACE. Yes. It's true.

(MARLO takes a moment then slowly, lowers his gun. He turns back to GRACE and moves towards her.)

GRACE. I... I'm sorry. I lied to you and I'm sorry you got put away. I didn't think it would end up as bad as this, and—

MARLO. *(gently)* Hey, hey. Take it easy. *(holds her)* I'm not mad at'cha.

GRACE. No?

MARLO. Course not. Fact, I'm glad you told me.

GRACE. *(almost sobbing)* You are?

MARLO. It's...it's the only way I'm gonna be able to do what I have to.

(**GRACE** *struggles to break free, but* **MARLO** *manages to put her in a choke hold.* **BRUCE** *runs towards them.*)

MARLO. Don't you move!

BRUCE. Marlo, please...

(He points the gun at **BRUCE**.*)*

MARLO. I told you it was like lying, didn't I? I *told you* what this could be.

(A loud smoker's cough can be heard from the auger floor.)

BRUCE. What was that?

MARLO. I told you. It's just the floor.

BRUCE. I swear, I just heard—

(The sound of whistling comes from the auger floor. The sound is clear, lively and comes without a hint of strain.)

GRACE. I don't think that's floor...

(The whistling continues.)

MARLO. *(pointing the gun)* Get up there. Both a' you.

(**BRUCE** *climbs the ladder and steps onto the walkway, followed by* **GRACE**.*)*

MARLO. What is it?

BRUCE. I can't see. You have to—

(**MARLO** *hits the lights. We now see that the sound of* **DAVEY***'s whistling is coming from the stereo system which is now resting on top of the walkway.* **MARLO** *climbs up the ladder.* **BRUCE** *holds up the stereo.*)

BRUCE. You know what this means? He might actually be... I mean, he might *actually be*...

MARLO. Smart.

BRUCE. *(stopping the tape)* He's not *smart*.

MARLO. That's two times now! Kid's like the fucking roadrunner.

BRUCE. Can you put the gun down?

MARLO. This doesn't change anything. She's still gonna talk.

BRUCE. If you kill her they'll know we did it for sure.

MARLO. Not if she an' Davey go missing at the same time. With that note and what happened to Spoza, they'll figure it a kidnapping for sure.

BRUCE. Maybe he heard us. Davey could be down at the police station right now.

MARLO. Just said yourself the kid ain't smart. Nah, he'll be back any minute now. *(beat)* You're gonna wanna turn around for this.

BRUCE. No.

(**BRUCE** *blocks his path.*)

MARLO. What are you doing?

BRUCE. The story doesn't work if you kill me too.

MARLO. If you had these kinda balls to begin with, I would never hadda to kill the wrong guy.

(**MARLO** *shoots* **BRUCE** *in the foot.* **BRUCE** *screams and drops to the ground, grabbing his foot.* **MARLO** *steps over him, moving towards* **GRACE**.)

GRACE. Marlo, please...

MARLO. I'm sorry, sweetheart.

(**MARLO** *cocks the pistol, pointing the gun at her head. His arms shake as he prepares to shoot.*)

BRUCE. I *knew.*

MARLO. *(still focused on* **GRACE***)* What?

BRUCE. *(rising)* I knew everything. The lawyer? Worst guy in town. You know what else? I'm the one who let it happen. Me.

MARLO. You're lying. You just said—

BRUCE. You think I actually give a shit about you? Drunk little daddy's boy, never does anything 'cept what he's told? Oh, yeah, I *really* give a fuck if you get sent away to the—

(**MARLO** *shoots* **BRUCE** *in the stomach.* **GRACE** *rushes* **MARLO**, *shoving him off the ramp and down into the augers. The sound of a heavy metalic thud.*)

MARLO. *(offstage)* Brothers man... Fuckin' *brothers*!

(*The sound of more gunshots being fired from behind the auger walls.* **GRACE** *ducks down to avoid the shots. He fires twice more.*)

BRUCE. *(gesturing towards the button)* Grace...Press the...You have...to press...the...

(**GRACE** *crawls over to the button and presses it. Just as she does this, the crawlspace door is pushed outward and* **MARLO** *begins to slowly make his way out. The sound of a loud buzzer.*)

MARLO. Oh...shit.

(**MARLO** *screams and is quickly pulled back into the crawlspace. The sound of the augers beginning to rotate, followed by loud crunching sounds. After a few moments,* **GRACE** *presses the stop button, bringing the sounds to a halt. She walks over to* **BRUCE**'*s body.*)

GRACE. Bruce, are you? *(She checks his pulse.)* Oh, Bruce...

(*She embraces* **BRUCE**'*s dead body. The sound of a door slamming.* **DAVEY** *enters from the hallway on the right side of the stage, whistling. He opens the crawlspace leading to the augers and enters headfirst.*)

DAVEY. *(offstage)* What the– Oh my god, oh my god, oh my god!

(**DAVEY**, *now covered in blood, squeezes out from the crawlspace door. He runs towards the breakroom.*)

Mr. Cafferty? Mr. Cafferty, there's been an accident! I just went to get some smokes and—*(sees the dog wrapped in tarp)* Baby?

(**DAVEY** *walks over to Baby and starts to cry.* **GRACE** *rests* **BRUCE**'*s body on the ground and begins to make* *her way down the ladder.* **DAVEY** *picks up the phone and dials three numbers.)*

DAVEY. Hello? I need an ambulance over at TroughKing. It...it's happened again.

*(***DAVEY** *drops the phone.* **GRACE** *descends from the ladder. She walks over to* **DAVEY** *and touches his shoulder.)*

DAVEY. Grace? Have you seen Mr. Cafferty?

GRACE. He's dead.

DAVEY. No, not him. Bruce.

*(***GRACE** *sighs and points towards the ladder)*

*(***DAVEY** *climbs the ladder. He sees* **BRUCE**'*s body and gently nudges him with his foot. He returns down the ladder. Pause.)*

DAVEY. Everything I Know Is Dead.

GRACE. Me too.

(Pause.)

DAVEY. *(He hands her a piece of paper.)* Here.

GRACE. What's this?

DAVEY. My receipt. That way you know it wasn't—

GRACE. That's okay. I saw everything. They were trying to kill you.

DAVEY. Me?

GRACE. Same way they did Gary.

DAVEY. Why?

GRACE. I don't know. Money?

DAVEY. But they're the richest people I know.

(Pause.)

GRACE. Is that, um...is...that Baby?

DAVEY. Yeah...

GRACE. I'm sorry. She's beautiful.

DAVEY. She *were*.

GRACE. You sure did a nice job on these tattoos.

DAVEY. Thanks.

GRACE. Maybe after we get this all figured out you can go ahead and do me.

DAVEY. Do you?

GRACE. With the tattoo gun.

DAVEY. Right. I was just...*(beat)* I'd like that. Hey, maybe we could go an' get the same one?

GRACE. Maybe. You got any smokes?

DAVEY. Just bought some. Here. *(disappointed)* Oh...

GRACE. What?

DAVEY. They're cloves...

GRACE. That's okay. I'll manage.

*(**DAVEY** takes a cigarette for himself and hands one to **GRACE**. They each put one in their mouths as **DAVEY** opens his lighter. In unison, they both lean forward towards the fire. The stage lights fade as their embers continue to glow.)*

End of Play

www.ingramcontent.com/pod-product-compliance
Lightning Source LLC
Chambersburg PA
CBHW071411290426
44108CB00014B/1780